THE

Engineer's, Millwright's and Machinist's PRACTICAL ASSISTANT;

COMPRISING

A COLLECTION OF USEFUL TABLES, RULES, AND DATA,

COMPILED AND ARRANGED,

WITH ORIGINAL MATTER,

BY

WILLIAM TEMPLETON,

AUTHOR OF "THE OPERATIVE MECHANIC'S WORKSHOP COMPANION," ETC. ETC.

SECOND EDITION.

H.M.S. SHIP "WARRIOR," 40 GUNS.

Extreme Length......	420 feet	Extreme Depth......	42 feet.
,, Breadth......	58 ,,	Tonnage	6117 tons.

Engines of 1250 Horse Power.

LONDON:

LOCKWOOD & CO., 7, STATIONERS' HALL COURT.

1862.

LONDON:

T. HARRILD, PRINTER, SHOE LANE,

FLEET STREET.

PREFACE.

Year after year, numerous new and many reconstructed books are introduced to public notice, some for useful information, more for idle recreation, but very few indeed for practical purposes connected with skilled knowledge in mechanical pursuits.

On my return to England recently, after an absence of nearly ten years in foreign countries—where works of practical utility on mechanical requirements could not be obtained, nor even heard of—I was astonished to find that my own compilations, published more than thirty years ago, were works still called for by the public, and it therefore occurred to me that a new compilation, embodying, in a concise form, the results of my long practice in various parts of the world, might obtain a share of public appreciation, and be of considerable value to those to whom it is dedicated.

With these views, and by the advice and entreaties

of many connected with the various branches of the Iron Trades, I issued circulars to that effect, whereby to ascertain the public feeling as to whether a work of the kind was now required; and, to my great satisfaction, I was inundated by orders for the work from all quarters. And now that it is in the hands of the public, I have only further to observe that it has been written partly for instruction, and partly for useful reference by those who are of necessity compelled to give a ready answer to any mechanical or engineering question.

The instructive portion of the work will no doubt be but little required; but I have been induced to comply with a number of solicitations from juniors in various professions, and I hope that such infringement will be forgiven by those of maturer years who are perfectly acquainted in practice with the rules of Decimal Arithmetic, now so generally employed.

London, 18 *Feb*. 1862.

PROPORTIONS FOR THE CONSTRUCTION OF TOOTHED WHEELS.

Pitch of Teeth devided into 15 equal parts.
From pitch circle to points of teeth 5 1/2 parts.
Length of teeth 12 parts
Working depth 11 „
Thickness of teeth 7 „
Spaee between 8 „
Breadth on face in ordinary cases
2 1/2 times the length of teeth.

1/2
5/8
3/4
7/8
1 in
1 1/8
1 1/4
1 3/8
1 1/2
1 5/8
1 3/4
1 7/8
2
2 1/8
2 1/4
2 3/8
2 1/2
2 5/8
2 3/4
2 7/8
3
3 1/8
3 1/4
3 3/8
3 1/2

Points of Teeth

Pitch Circle

0 1 2 3 4 5 6 7 8 9 10 11 12

Length of Teeth.

Kell Bro^s Lith^rs Castle St Holborn

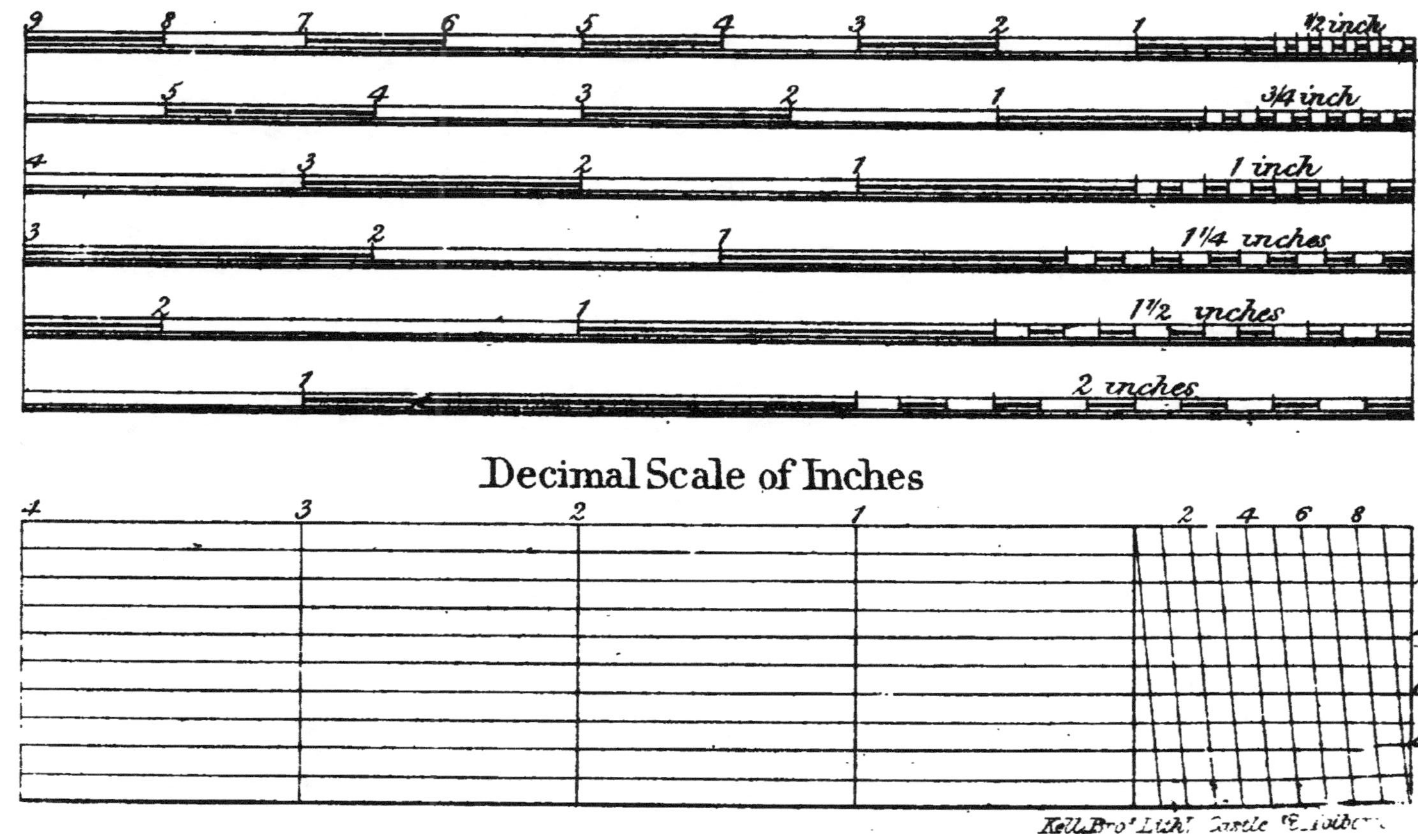
Scales of Feet and Inches.
1/2 inch
3/4 inch
1 inch
1 1/4 inches
1 1/2 inches
2 inches
Decimal Scale of Inches

THE

Engineer's, Millwright's, & Machinist's

PRACTICAL ASSISTANT.

DEFINITIONS OF ARITHMETICAL SIGNS AS IN COMMON USE.

$=$ Sign of Equality, and signifies equal to, as 7 added to 6 $= 13$.

$+$ " Addition, signifies plus or more, as $7 + 8 = 15$.

$-$ " Subtraction, " minus or less, as $14 - 5 = 9$.

$\times$ " Multiplication, " multiply by, as $12 \times 5 = 60$.

$\div$ " Division, " divide by, as $16 \div 4 = 4$. or, $\frac{16}{4} = 4$.

$: \; :: \; :$ Proportion, " as 4 is to 8, so is 12 to 24.

$\sqrt{}$ Sign of Square Root, $\sqrt[3]{}$ " Cube Root, " evolution, or the extraction of roots, as $\sqrt{64} = 8$, and $\sqrt[3]{64} = 4$.

6^2 " To be squared, 6^3 " To be cubed, " involution, or the raising of powers; $6^2 = 36$, and $6^3 = 216$.

$\overline{7 + 5} \times 6 = 72$ signifies line or bar, as 7 added to 5 $= 12$, and 12 multiplied by 6 $= 72$.

$\sqrt{5^2 - 3^2} = 4$ " that 3 squared taken from 5 squared, the square root of the remainder $= 4$.

$\sqrt[3]{\frac{20 \times 12}{30}} = 2$ " that 20 multiplied by 12 and the product divided by 30, the cube root of the quotient $= 2$.

STANDARD WEIGHTS AND MEASURES OF GREAT BRITAIN AND ITS COLONIES.

THE IMPERIAL MEASURES INTRODUCED JANUARY 1st, 1826.

Avoirdupois, or Commercial Weight.

		MARK.
·10831 cubic inches of pure water, at 62° Fahrenheit, or 27·34375 grs. troy	= 1 dram,	*dr.*
16 drams	= 1 ounce,	*oz.*
16 ounces	= 1 pound,	*lb.*
14 pounds	= 1 stone,	*st.*
2 stones, or 28 pounds	= 1 quarter,	*qr.*
4 quarters, or 112 pounds ...	= 1 hundred-weight,	*cwt.*
20 hundred-weights, or 2,240 pounds	= 1 ton,	*T.*

NOTE.—The stone is principally used in weighing Hay, Straw, and Live Cattle, and commonly called Jockey Weight.

Troy Weight

Is used in weighing Gold, Silver, and Precious Stones, and also in estimating the results of Philosophical experiments.

		MARK.
1·901306 cubic inches of pure water, at 62° Fahrenheit ...	= 480 grains,	*gr.*
24 grains	= 1 pennyweight,	*dwt.*
20 pennyweights	= 1 ounce,	*oz.*
12 ounces	= 1 pound,	*lb.*

NOTE.—Avoirdupois lbs. × 1·21528 = Troy lbs.
„ oz. × ·9115 = „ oz.
Troy lbs. × ·823 = Avoi. lbs.
„ ozs. × 1·1 = „ ozs.
„ grs. × ·03657 = „ drs.

Lineal Measures, or Measures of Length.

The English Standard Yard of 1760, and now lodged in the custody of the Clerk of the House of Commons, is made the standard or unit for all measures of extension whatsoever, and $\frac{1}{36}$ of such yard = 1 inch.

7·92 inches		= 1 link.
12 ,,		= 1 foot.
3 feet		= 1 yard.
6 feet		= 1 fathom.
16½ ,, or 5½ yards		= 1 rod, pole, or perch.
792 inches	}	= 1 chain.
66 feet	}	
22 yards, or 4 poles	}	
220 yards	}	= 1 furlong.
40 poles, or	}	
10 chains	}	
5280 feet	}	= 1 statute mile.
1760 yards	}	
320 poles	}	
80 chains, or	}	
8 furlongs	}	
6082·6 feet, or	}	= 1 nautical mile.
2027·5 yards	}	

Mean diameter of the Earth=7920·5 English statute miles.
Circumference of the Earth=24883 miles, or 43794000 yds.
Curvature of the Earth=7·962 inches per mile.

The fathom is chiefly used for seafaring and mining purposes. 8 fathoms = the length of the Navy log-line, and 120 fathoms = a cable's length.

Square, or Superficial Measures.

144 square inches		= 1 square foot.
9 ,, feet		= 1 ,, yard.
272¼ ,, feet, or	}	= 1 pole or perch.
30¼ ,, yards	}	
40 poles		= 1 rood.
4840 square yards, or	}	= 1 acre.
10 ,, chains	}	
640 acres		= 1 square mile.

Cubic Measures, or Measures of Solidity and Capacity.

1728 cubic inches	= 1 cubic foot.	
27 „ feet	= 1 „ yard.	
5 „ feet	= 1 barrel bulk of shipping.	
42 „ feet	= 1 ton of shipping.	
A load of unhewn timber	= 40 cubic feet.	
„ squared „	= 50 „	
A cord of wood	= 128 „	

Imperial Measures of Capacity, for all Liquids, Grain, and other Dry Goods.

5 ozs. Avoir. of pure water at 62° Fahrenheit	= 1 gill	=	8·665 cubic in.
4 gills	= 1 pint	=	34·659 „
2 pints	= 1 quart	=	69·318 „
4 quarts	= 1 gallon	=	277·274 „
2 gallons	= 1 peck	=	554·548 „
4 pecks	= 1 bushel	=	2218·192 „
8 bushels	= 1 quarter	=	10·27 cubic feet.

NOTE.—The peck, bushel, and quarter are for dry goods only.

Formerly the Wine gallon contained 231, the Ale gallon 282, and the bushel measure 2150·42 cubic inches.

1 peck of flour	= 14 lbs. Avoir.		
1 bushel „	= 56 „ „		
1 barrel „	= 196 „ „	or 1¾ cwt.	
1 sack „	= 280 „ „	„ 2½ „	

Special Wine Measures.

10 gallons	= 1 anker.
18 „	= 1 runlet.
42 „	= 1 tierce.
63 „	= 1 hogshead.
84 „	= 1 puncheon
126 „	= 1 pipe.
252 „	= 1 tun.

Special Ale and Beer Measures.

9 gallons	= 1 firkin.
18 „	= 1 kilderkin.
36 „	= 1 barrel.
54 „	= 1 hogshead.
72 „	= 1 puncheon
108 „	= 1 butt.

Although thus classified, they are, in trading, generally

gauged, and bought or sold in accordance with the number of Imperial gallons therein contained. One cubic foot is equal to 6¼ Imperial gallons.

Dimensions of Imperial Conical Liquid Measures.

	DIAMETERS.				DEPTHS.
Gill	top	⅝ inch,	bottom	2⅞	3·166 inches.
Half-pint	„	⅞ „	„	3½	4·117 „
Pint	„	1 „	„	4½	5·141 „
Quart	„	1¼ „	„	5¾	6·332 „
Half-gallon	„	1¾ „	„	7	8·234 „
Gallon	„	2 inches,	„	9	10·282 „
Two-gallon	„	2½ „	„	11½	12·665 „

Dimensions of Imperial Cylindrical Dry Measures (not heaped).

DEPTHS EQUAL TO THE DIAMETERS.

Eighth of a peck,	a cylinder of	4·452 inches.
Forpit, or half-gallon	„	5·609 „
Gallon, or half-peck	„	7·067 „
Peck	„	8·904 „
Half-bushel	„	11·219 „
Bushel	„	14·135 „
Quarter	„	28·270 „

Dimensions of Cylindrical heaped Measures, for Coke, Lime, Fish, Fruit, Potatoes, &c.

Half-gallon	= 7¾ inches diameter	= 176	Cubic inches when the measures are heaped.
Gallon	= 9¾ „ „	= 352	
Peck	= 12¼ „ „	= 704	
Half-bushel	= 15½ „ „	= 1407¾	
Bushel	= 19½ „ „	= 2815½	
3 bushels	= 1 sack, and	= 4·889 cubic feet.	
12 sacks	= 1 chaldron	= 58·656 „ „	

Note.—The Act directs that the depth of each measure shall not exceed half its diameter, and the height of the cone or heap at least three-fourths of its depth.

Previous to 1835, coals were bought and sold by heaped measures. The bushel was supposed to contain 80 lbs. Avoirdupois, and 28 such bushels to equal 1 ton; but in that year an Act was passed which abolished the sytem. Now they are estimated by the cwt., or 112 lbs. Avoirdupois, 224 lbs. being 1 sack, and 10 such sacks equal 1 ton.

The average mean weight of different kinds of coal, broken up and properly prepared as practical fuel, is 50 lbs. per cubic foot, and 45 cubic feet the stowage capacity per ton.

NOTE.—The reason why I here introduce abolished or antiquated coal measures, is because the units of work done by steam-engines were estimated formerly from the consumption of coals by the bushel; now that units of work done is valued by the lb. of coal, comparison of results is not unfrequently required.

FRENCH WEIGHTS AND MEASURES,

AS MOST FREQUENTLY REQUIRED FOR ENGLISH COMPARISONS.

Weights.

1 milligramme = ·015438 English Troy grains.
1 gramme = 15·438 " " "
or ·002205 of a lb. Avoirdupois.
1 kilogramme = 2·2048 lbs. Avoirdupois.

WEIGHTS AS POPULARLY ESTIMATED.

		lbs.	ozs.	drs. Avoirdupois.
1 gramme	=	0	0	0½
1 decagramme.........	=	0	0	5¾
1 hectogramme	=	0	3	8¼
1 kilogramme	=	2	3	4⅛

Lineal Measures.

1 millimetre	=	·039371	English	inches.
25½ "	=	1	"	inch.
1 metre	=	39 371 or 39⅜	"	inches.
or	=	3·2809 feet = 3 feet 3⅜ inches.		

Measures of Surface.

1 centiare	=	1·196 English sq. yds., or 10·764 English [square feet.
9·3 centiares	=	100 „ „ feet.
1 are	=	119·6 „ „ yards.
40·47 ares	=	1 „ statute acre.
1 hectare	=	2·47 „ „

Measures of Solidity.

1 millistere .... = ·035317 English cubic feet.
1 stere .... = 35·317 „ „

Measures of Capacity.

1 litre .... = 61·028 English cubic inches.

POPULAR MEASURES OF CAPACITY.

		English galls.	qts.	pts. Imp.
1 litre	=	0	0	1¾ „
1 decalitre	=	2	0	1½ „
1 hectolitre	=	22	0	0
1 kilolitre	=	220	0	0

Conversion of Equivalent Measures.

English to French.			French to English.	
Inches ...	× ·0254	= metres	× 39·371	= inches.
Feet	× ·30477	= „	× 3·2809	= feet.
Yards ...	× ·91438	= „	× 1·09364	= yards.
Miles	× 1·6093	= kilometres...	× ·62138	= miles.
Acres	× ·40467	= hectares......	× 2·4712	= acres.
Imp. galls.	× 4·54339	= litres	× ·2201	= gallons.
Cubic ins.	× ·01639	= „	× 61·028	= cubic ins.
Bushels .	× ·36347	= hectolitres .	× 2·75125	= bushels.
Quarters .	× 2·9077	= „ .	× ·3439	= quarters.
Troy grs. .	× ·06479	= grammes ...	× 15·434	= Troy grs.
Troy lbs. .	× ·3732	= kilogrammes	× 2·6795	= Troy lbs.
Avoir. lbs.	× ·4535	= „	× 2·2048	= Avoir. lbs.

ON SIMPLE ARITHMETIC;

WITH REDUCED VULGAR FRACTIONS, COMMONLY CALLED DECIMAL ARITHMETIC.

Vulgar Fractions signify a part or parts of any whole unit, of whatever description; thus, one mile is a unit, and one yard is a fraction of it; one foot is a unit, and one inch is a fraction of it, &c. Hence, fractions may be portions of some known weight, measure, capacity, or any thing else. Practically 1 pound Avoirdupois contains, or is equal to, 16 ounces, consequently 4 ounces equal $\frac{1}{4}$, or fraction of a pound. In lineal measure, 12 inches equal one foot; then 6 inches equal $\frac{1}{2}$. Again, 32 gills equal 1 gallon, therefore 24 gills equal $\frac{3}{4}$, such being simple fractions vulgarly expressed. The lower figures are called the denominators of the fraction, because they express or represent the number of parts into which the unit is divided; and the upper figures are called the numerators of the fraction, because they show the number of those fractional parts taken into account. But calculations by vulgar fractions are both tedious and difficult, compared with decimal fractions, and chiefly because of the various scales employed in measurements and established modes of reckoning quantities hitherto in common use; hence the utility of decimal arithmetic, whose fractions are uniformly tenths, hundredths, thousandths, &c., which simply may be construed from vulgar fractions, and so rendered practically equivalent to suit any purpose required.

Rule by which to reduce vulgar fractions to decimals of equal value.—Add a cipher or ciphers on the right hand of the numerator for a dividend, and divide by the denominator, and if any significant figure or figures remain in the dividend, annex a cipher as before, and so continue until all significant figures are terminated in the dividend. But some vulgar fractions will not come to a termination as decimals; however, when such is the case three or four decimal figures in the quotient are of quite sufficient exactitude in practical estimations.

Examples for Elucidation.

1 Reduce $\frac{1}{4}$ of a lb. Avoirdupois to a decimal of equal value.

```
Divisor.  Dividend.  Quotient.
   4 )      1·0      ( ·25 the answer.
             8
            ---
            20
            20
            ===

Or, 4/16.     16 ) 4·0 ( ·25  Answer as before.
                   32
                   ---
                    80
                    80
                   ===
```

2. Reduce $\frac{3}{4}$ of an Imperial gallon to an equivalent decimal.

```
4 ) 3·0 ( ·75     Or, 24/32.  32 ) 24·0 ( ·75
    28                             224
    ---                            ---
     20                            160
     20                            160
    ===                            ===
```

3. Reduce 17 inches to the decimal of a yard of 36 inches.

```
17/36   36 ) 17·0 ( ·4722  Not terminated, but
             144             sufficiently near the
             ---             truth.
             260
             252
             ---
               80
               72
              ---
               80
               72
              ---
                8
              ===
```

In the first and second examples two ciphers are added in the dividend of each, consequently the quotients consist of two decimals each; and in the third example four ciphers are added, hence four decimals in the quotient.

All decimal quotients must be notified by a dot close to the left hand figure, by which they may be distinguished from whole numbers, when specially annexed.

Table of Notation and Numeration for whole Numbers and Decimals.

Millions.	Hundreds of Thousands.	Tens of Thousands.	Thousands.	Hundreds.	Tens.	Units.	Dot, or Decimal point.	Tenths.	Hundredths.	Thousandths.	Tenths of Thousandths.	Hundredths of Thousandths.	Millionths.
7	6	5	4	3	2	1	•	1	2	3	4	5	6

Whole numbers increase in value from right to left by tens, and decimals diminish in value from left to right in an equal ratio. Thus, the three first figures from the decimal point in whole numbers equal 321, and the three first figures from the decimal point in decimals is ·123 thousandths. Replace the unit in whole numbers by a cipher, and the sum is 320; replace the 1 or tenth in decimals by a cipher, and the sum is 23 thousandths. Again, replace the tens in whole numbers by a cipher, and the sum is 300; but replace the hundredths in decimals by a cipher, and the sum is reduced to 3 thousandth parts of the unit or whole number, and each sum would stand numerically thus:—321·123, 320·023, and 300·003. Hence, it will be observed that ciphers annexed on the right hand of whole numbers do not change the value of those on the left; but in decimals, ciphers added on the left hand of significant figures, reduce the value of the sum in a tenfold proportion with the number of ciphers annexed, and ciphers on the right hand of significant figures in decimals are of no value whatever.

To reduce decimal sums to vulgar fractions of equal value.

RULE.—Multiply any decimal, or number of decimals, and of whatever denomination, by the next lower division or gradation of its scale in value; count off from the right hand of the product as many figures for decimals as there are decimals in the multiplier and multiplicand together, then place the decimal point immediately after the last figure; again, multiply the remaining decimals by the next lower division in its scale of value, and so proceed, as before, until no further decimals remain in the multiplicand, or until no lower division is necessary to be taken into account.

Ex. 1. What is the value vulgarly, as in common practice, of the decimal ·46875 of a lineal inch?

	·46875	the multiplicand.
	× 8	or eighths, the multiplier.
1st Pro.	3·75000	
	× 2	two-sixteenths equal one-eighth.
2nd Pro.	1·50	
	× 2	two 32s equal $\frac{1}{16}$.
	1·0	Hence the value of the decimal is $\frac{3}{8}$, $\frac{1}{16}$, and $\frac{1}{32}$ of an inch.

Ex. 2. Required, the common fractions of a foot whose decimal is ·32292.

·32292	
× 12	twelve inches equal 1 foot.
3·87504	
× 8	eighths equal 1 inch.
7·00032	Answer, 3 inches and $\frac{7}{8}$, with a remainder of 32 thousandth parts of an inch.

Ex. 3. What is the value of ·3875 of a £ sterling?

·3875	
× 20	shillings equal £1.
7·7500	
× 12	pence equal 1 shilling.
9·0000	Answer, 7 shillings and 9 pence.

NOTE.—It being quite unnecessary to retain ciphers on the right hand of significant figures as decimals in the multiplicand, they are in consequence either retained or thrown away at pleasure in the working of the question.

The four fundamental rules of decimal arithmetic, viz., Addition, Subtraction, Multiplication, and Division, are precisely those of common arithmetic, with the exception of placing the decimal or separating point, which must be duly attended to, in accordance with the previous instructions given, and little more is necessary than an example or two, merely to impress them upon the memory more permanently, and as a reference at any time when they may be required.

IN ADDITION.

Ex. Add together the following whole numbers and decimals.

```
 23·701
 14·014
102·001
 17·413
  5·5
  8·191
-------
170·820
```

170·820 Total sum, equal one hundred and seventy as whole numbers, and eight-tenths and two hundredths, or eighty-two hundredths, as decimals.

In Subtraction.

Subtract 477·9241 from 9001·246.

```
9001·246
 477·9241
─────────
8523·3219  Remainder.
```

In Multiplication.

Multiply 48·74 by 2·67.

```
  2·67
───────
  34118
 29244
 9748
───────
130·1358  Product.
```

In the multiplication of decimals by decimals alone it sometimes occurs that the product will not contain so many figures as the multiplier and multiplicand together, as per rule; consequently a cipher or ciphers must be annexed on the left hand of the product, so as to reduce it to its proper terms.

Ex. Multiply ·125 by ·031.

```
   ·125
   ·031
───────
    125
   375
───────
·003875
```

In this product 6 decimals are required, hence 2 ciphers are annexed to make the proper reduced value.

In Division.

Divide 853·007 by 92·142.

```
92·142 ) 853·007 ( 9·2575
         829278
         ------
          237290
          184284
          ------
           530060
           460710
           ------
            693500
            644994
            ------
             485060
             460710
             ------
              24350 &c.
```

To ascertain the number of figures that must be pointed off in the quotient for decimals, count the number in the dividend, then the number in the divisor and quotient together must equal those of the dividend. In this question there are 7 decimals in the dividend and 3 in the divisor; then 3 from 7 leaves 4 to be cut off in the quotient.

Divide 1 by 42·872.

In such cases as this, as many ciphers must be added to the 1 whereby to form a dividend as there are figures in the divisor; hence the dividend stands thus:—

```
42·872 ) 1·00000 ( ·02309
          85744
          ------
          142560
          138616
          ------
           394400
           385848
           ------
             8552 &c.
```

In this there are 8 decimals in the dividend, and 3 in th divisor, consequently 5 in the quotient.

The following tables of Decimal equivalents are here subjoined, in order to obviate the constant necessity for reduction of vulgar fractions to decimals of almost daily practical wants.

Tables of Decimal Equivalents to Fractional parts of Lineal Measures British.

1 Inch = Unity, and divided into 32 parts.

	Are equal to		Are equal to		Are equal to
·96875	$\frac{7}{8}$ & $\frac{3}{32}$	·625	$\frac{5}{8}$	·28125	$\frac{1}{4}$ & $\frac{1}{32}$
·9375	$\frac{7}{8}$ & $\frac{1}{16}$	·59375	$\frac{1}{2}$ & $\frac{3}{32}$	·25	$\frac{1}{4}$
·90625	$\frac{7}{8}$ & $\frac{1}{32}$	·5625	$\frac{1}{2}$ & $\frac{1}{16}$	·21875	$\frac{1}{8}$ & $\frac{3}{32}$
·875	$\frac{7}{8}$	·53125	$\frac{1}{2}$ & $\frac{1}{32}$	·1875	$\frac{1}{8}$ & $\frac{1}{16}$
·84375	$\frac{3}{4}$ & $\frac{3}{32}$	·5	$\frac{1}{2}$	·15625	$\frac{1}{8}$ & $\frac{1}{32}$
·8125	$\frac{3}{4}$ & $\frac{1}{16}$	·46875	$\frac{3}{8}$ & $\frac{3}{32}$	·125	$\frac{1}{8}$
·78125	$\frac{3}{4}$ & $\frac{1}{32}$	·4375	$\frac{3}{8}$ & $\frac{1}{16}$	·09375	$\frac{3}{32}$
·75	$\frac{3}{4}$	·40625	$\frac{3}{8}$ & $\frac{1}{32}$	·6625	$\frac{1}{16}$
·71875	$\frac{5}{8}$ & $\frac{3}{32}$	·375	$\frac{3}{8}$	·03125	$\frac{1}{32}$
·6875	$\frac{5}{8}$ & $\frac{1}{16}$	·34375	$\frac{1}{4}$ & $\frac{3}{32}$	·015625	$\frac{1}{64}$
·65625	$\frac{5}{8}$ & $\frac{1}{32}$	·3125	$\frac{1}{4}$ & $\frac{1}{16}$	·0078125	$\frac{1}{128}$

1 Foot = Unity, and divided into 48 parts.

	Are equal to		Are equal to		Are equal to
·9791	$11\frac{3}{4}$	·62497	$7\frac{1}{2}$	·27083	$3\frac{1}{4}$
·95827	$11\frac{1}{2}$	·60313	$7\frac{1}{4}$	·25	3
·93748	$11\frac{1}{4}$	·5833	7	·2291	$2\frac{3}{4}$
·9166	11	·5625	$6\frac{3}{4}$	·20827	$2\frac{1}{2}$
·8958	$10\frac{3}{4}$	·54167	$6\frac{1}{2}$	·18743	$2\frac{1}{4}$
·87497	$10\frac{1}{2}$	·52083	$6\frac{1}{4}$	·1666	2
·85413	$10\frac{1}{4}$	·5	6	·1458	$1\frac{3}{4}$
·8333	10	·4791	$5\frac{3}{4}$	·12497	$1\frac{1}{2}$
·8125	$9\frac{3}{4}$	·45827	$5\frac{1}{2}$	·10413	$1\frac{1}{4}$
·79167	$9\frac{1}{2}$	·43743	$5\frac{1}{4}$	·0833	1
·77083	$9\frac{1}{4}$	·4166	5	·07292	$\frac{7}{8}$
·75	9	·3958	$4\frac{3}{4}$	·0625	$\frac{3}{4}$
·7291	$8\frac{3}{4}$	·37497	$4\frac{1}{2}$	·05208	$\frac{5}{8}$
·70827	$8\frac{1}{2}$	·35413	$4\frac{1}{4}$	·04167	$\frac{1}{2}$
·68723	$8\frac{1}{4}$	·3333	4	·03125	$\frac{3}{8}$
·6666	8	·3125	$3\frac{3}{4}$	·02083	$\frac{1}{4}$
·6458	$7\frac{3}{4}$	·29167	$3\frac{1}{2}$	·01042	$\frac{1}{8}$

1 Yard = Unity, and divided into 36 parts.

Decimal		Parts	Decimal		Parts	Decimal		Parts
·9722	Are equal to	35	·6389	Are equal to	23	·3055	Are equal to	11
·9444		34	·6111		22	·2778		10
·9167		33	·5833		21	·25		9
·8889		32	·5556		20	·2222		8
·8611		31	·5278		19	·1944		7
·8333		30	·5		18	·1667		6
·8056		29	·4722		17	·1389		5
·7778		28	·4444		16	·1111		4
·75		27	·4167		15	·0833		3
·7222		26	·3889		14	·0555		2
·6944		25	·3611		13	·0278		1
·6667		24	·3333		12	·01389		½

1 Pound Avoirdupois=Unity, and divided into 16 parts: 16 drams = 1 oz., and 16 ozs. = 1 pound.

Decimal				Decimal			
·0625	= 1	dram,	or oz.	·5625	= 9	drams,	or ozs.
·125	= 2	"	"	·625	= 10	"	"
·1875	= 3	"	"	·6875	= 11	"	"
·25	= 4	"	"	·75	= 12	"	"
·3125	= 5	"	"	·8125	= 13	"	"
·375	= 6	"	"	·875	= 14	"	"
·4375	= 7	"	"	·9375	= 15	"	"
·5	= 8	"	"	1 oz. or lb.	= 16	"	"

Common Fractions, with Decimal Equivalents.

$\frac{1}{4} = \frac{2}{8} = \frac{3}{12}$ .... = ·25	$\frac{1}{5}$ = ·2
$\frac{1}{3} = \frac{2}{6} = \frac{3}{9}$ .... = ·333	$\frac{1}{6}$ = ·1666
$\frac{1}{2} = \frac{2}{4} = \frac{3}{6} = \frac{4}{8} = \frac{6}{12}$ = ·5	$\frac{1}{7}$ = ·1428
$\frac{2}{3} = \frac{4}{6} = \frac{6}{9}$ .... = ·666	$\frac{1}{8}$ = ·125
$\frac{3}{4} = \frac{6}{8} = \frac{9}{12}$ .... = ·75	$\frac{1}{9}$ = ·111

Decimal Approximates for the facilitation of practical calculations in British Measures.

Avoirdupois lbs.	×	·009	= hundred-weights.
„ „	×	·00045	= tons.
Circum. of a circle...	×	·31831	= the diameter.
Circular inches	×	·00546	= square feet.
Cube of diam. of a sphere	×	·5236	= the solidity.
Cubic inches	×	·00058	= cubic feet.
„ feet	×	·03704	= „ yards.
„ inches	×	·003607	= Imperial gallons.
„ feet	×	6·232	= „ „
Cylindrical inches ...	×	·0004546	= cubic yards.
„ „ ...	×	·002832	= Imperial gallons.
„ feet	×	·02909	= cubic yards.
„ feet	×	4·895	= Imperial gallons.
Diam. of a circle ...	×	3·1416	= the circumference.
„ „ ...	×	·8862	= side of equal square.
„ „ ...	×	·7071	= side of inscribed sq.
Side of a square	×	1·4142	= dia. of circum. circle
Diam. of a sphere ...	×	·806	= dimensions of equal cube.
„ „ ...	×	·6667	= length of equal cylinder.
Lineal feet	×	·00019	= English statute miles
„ yards	×	·000568	= „ „ „
Side of a square	×	1·1284	= diameter of circle of equal area.
„ „	×	3·545	= circum. of circle of equal area.
Square of diameter...	×	·7854	= area of equal circle.
„ root of area...	×	1·12837	= diam. of equal circle.
„ inches	×	·00694	= square feet.
„ yards	×	·0002067	= English statute acres.
Sq. of dia. of a sphere	×	3·1416	= convex surface of a sphere.

183·346 circular inches equal 1 square foot.
2200 cylindrical inches equal 1 cubic foot.

Tables of Specific Gravities,

OR WEIGHTS OF BODIES WHOSE MAGNITUDES ARE EQUAL, BUT OF UNEQUAL DENSITIES.

One cubic foot of pure fresh water at 62° Fahrenheit = 1000 ounces Avoirdupois; hence it is conveniently, and with propriety, adopted as the standard of comparison by which the densities of other bodies are generally referred, and also the means by which to ascertain the densities of other bodies hitherto untabulated.

Atmospheric air = ·0768, or is 820 times lighter than water.

METALS.	Weight, water being 1000.	Cubic inches in lbs. Avoir.	Weight of 1 cub. in. in lbs.
Antimony, cast	4500	6·244	·16
Bismuth ,,	9810	2·818	·3545
Brass, average, ,,	8357	3·308	·3023
Bronze ,,	8459	3·268	·306
Cadmium	8600	—	—
Copper, cast	8667	3·19	·3135
,, wrought	8788	3·146	·3178
Gold, pure	19258	1·435	·6965
Gun-metal, cast	8561	3·23	·3096
Iron ,,	7244	3·814	·2622
,, bar	7701	3·592	·2792
,, wrought	7792	3·548	·282
Lead, cast	11352	2·435	·415
Mercury at 32° Fahrenheit	13619	—	—
,, 60° ,,	13580	2·035	·4914
,, 212° ,,	13375	—	—
Nickel	8270	3·342	·3
Platinum	20978	1·318	·759
Silver, pure	10474	2·638	·3788
Steel, soft	7780	3·554	·281
,, hardened	7840	3·527	·2835
Tin, cast	7291	3·79	·2636
Zinc, ,,	7190	3·845	·26

Various Bodies.	Sp. Gr.	Cub. ft. lbs.	Cub. feet = 1 T.
Brick, red, common	1684	105	21·4
„ fire, Welsh	1931	120·7	18·5
Burrs, French, average	2484	151	14
Clay, common	1920	120	18·7
Coal, average	1319	82·4	27·2
Coke, dry	755	47	47·6
Glass, plate	2453	153·3	14·6
Granite, average	2651	165·7	13·5
Gravel, „	1920	120	18·7
Ice, from fresh water	1001	53	35·5
Marble, average	2720	170	13
Salt, dry	2130	134·5	18
Sand, river	1520	95	25
Slate, average	2800	112·5	19·2
Sandstone, „	2350	147	15 2
Tallow, „	942	59	38

Liquids.	Sp. Gr.	Weight of Im. gal. lbs.	Weight of cub. in. lbs.
Alcohol of Commerce	825	8·2	·0296
„ Absolute	797	7·9	·0285
Acid, Sulphuric	1850	18·5	·0667
„ Nitric	1271	12·7	·0458
„ Muriatic	1200	12	·0433
„ Citric	1034	10·3	·0371
Ether, Nitric	908	9·1	·0328
„ Muriatic	729	7·3	·0263
Oil, Linseed	940	9·4	·0389
„ Olive	915	9·2	·0332
„ Rapeseed	919	9·3	·0335
„ Whale	923	9·4	·0339
Sea Water, average	1028	10·3	·0371
Spirits, proof	922	9·2	·0332
„ of Wine	830	8·3	·0299
Tar, from Wood	1015	10·1	·0364
Turpentine	870	8·7	·0314
Vinegar, distilled	1009	10	·0361
Wine, Bordeaux	994	9·94	·0358
„ Port	997	9·97	—

TIMBER, SEASONED.	Sp. Gr.	Pounds per cub. ft.	Cubic ft. = 1 Ton.
Alder	736	46	48¾
Apple-tree	792	49½	45¼
Ash	845	52	43
Beech	852	53¼	42
Birch, English	792	49½	45¼
„ black, American	648	40½	55
Blackwood, Australian	662	41⅜	54
Blue Gum, „	1100	68¾	32½
Box, French	1328	83	27
„ Dutch	912	57	39
Cedar, American	561	35	64
„ Sydney	560	34½	64
„ Canadian	910	57	39¼
Cherry-tree	715	45	50
Chestnut	610	38	59
Cork	240	15	149
Cowrie Pine, New Zealand	512	32	70
Crab-tree	768	48	46½
Ebony, Indian	1208	75½	29
„ American	1331	83	27
Elm	673	42	53
Hawthorn	610	38	59
Holly and Hornbeam, each	760	47½	47¼
Iron Bark, Australian	1233	77	29
Laburnum	920	57½	39
Lance-wood	1023	64	35
Larch	530	31	72¼
Lemon-tree	704	44	51
Lignum Vitæ	1336	83½	26½
Lime-tree	760	47½	47¼
Logwood	913	57	39½
Mahogany, Spanish	720	45	50
„ Honduras	560	35	64
Maple	752	47	47½
Oak, English	934	58	38⅓
„ American	672	42	53¼

TIMBER, SEASONED.	Sp. Gr.	Pounds per cub. ft.	Cubic ft. = 1 Ton.
Oak, African	944	59	38
Orange-tree	705	44	49¾
Pear-tree	660	41	54½
Pine, pitch	736	46	48¾
„ red	672	42	53
„ white	456	28½	78½
„ yellow	448	28	80
Poona	640	40	35
Poplar	384	24	93¼
Plum-tree	785	49	45¾
Red Gum, Australian	901	56	40
Rosewood, black	1280	80	28
Sycamore	624	39	57½
Teak	750	46	48½
Walnut	671	42	53½
Willow	585	36½	61¼
Yew, Spanish	807	50½	44¼
„ Dutch	788	49¼	45

Elastic Fluids or Gases, Atmospheric Air being 1000.

Gas	
Ammoniacal Gas	·500
Azote, or Nitrogen	·969
Carburetted Hydrogen	·491
Hydrogen	·074
Oxygen, mean	1·044
Steam of water at 212° Faht.	·690
Sulphuretted Hydrogen	1·777
Sulphurous Acid Gas	2·193
Vapour of Alcohol	2·100

Useful units of fresh water at a mean temperature.

			Avoir.					Avoir.	
1 cubic in.		=	·03617 lbs.	1 cylin. in.			=	·02842 lbs.	
12	„ ins.	=	·434 „	12	„	ins.	=	·341	„
1	„ foot	=	62·5 „	1	„	foot	=	49·1	„
1·8	„ feet	=	1 cwt.	2·282	„	feet	=	1 cwt.	
35·84	„ feet	=	1 ton.	45·64	„	feet	=	1 ton.	

27·648 cubic inches .... = 1 lb. Avoir.
1 gallon (Imperial) ...... = 10 „ „
11·2 gallons „ ...... = 1 cwt.
224 „ „ ...... = 1 ton.
277·274 cubic inches .... = 1 Imperial gallon.
12 „ „ ... = ·043284 „ „
1 „ inch ... = ·003607 „ „
1 „ foot .. = 6·232 „ gallons.
353 cylindrical inches = 1 Imperial gallon.
12 „ „ = ·034 „ „
1 „ „ = ·002832 „ „
1 „ foot = 4·895 „ gallons.

Sea water, average density.

26·895 cubic inches ...... = 1 lb. Avoir.
1 gallon (Imperial)...... = 10·25 „
10·93 „ „ ...... = 1 cwt.
218·6 „ „ ...... = 1 ton.
1 cubic foot .... = 64·2 lbs. Avoir.
34·9 „ feet .... = 1 ton.

Comparative densities and degrees of Saltness of Sea water from various localities, that of the British Channel being 1·00.

The Baltic Sea	= 0·19	At the Equator	= 1·12
The Black Sea	= 0·61	North Atlantic	= 1·16
The Irish Channel .	= 0·96	Sea of Marmora ...	= 1·18
The Mediteranneean	= 1·11	South Atlantic	= 1·20

The following Examples show the utility of the preceding Tables, viz., Decimal Equivalents, Decimal Approximates, and Decimal Weights of a cubic inch in Tables of Specific Gravities.

Ex. 1. Required, the superficial contents, in square feet of any right-lined figure whose breadth at one end equal 2 ft. $5\frac{3}{4}$ inches; at the other end 1 ft. $10\frac{1}{2}$ inches, and length 5 ft. $3\frac{1}{4}$ inches.

(See Tables of Decimal Equivalents, page 19.)

2·4791 = 2 feet $5\frac{3}{4}$ inches.
+ 1·87497 = 1 „ $10\frac{1}{2}$ „
÷ 2) 4·35407
2·177 mean breadth.
× 5·27 = 5 feet $3\frac{1}{4}$ inches.
15239
4354
10885
11·47279 ft. superficial surface.

Again: 2 feet $5\frac{3}{4}$ inches = 29·75 inches.
and 1 foot $10\frac{1}{2}$ „ = + 22·5 „
÷ 2) 52·25
Mean breadth 26·125
5 feet $3\frac{1}{4}$ inches = × 63·25
130625
52250
78375
156750
Square inches 1652·4|0625
(See Table, page 21.) × ·00694 or, ·007
66096
148716
99144
Square feet nearly 11·467656 as before.

Ex. 2. A piece of wood as a pattern for a casting of iron $15\frac{7}{16}$ inches in length, $7\frac{1}{8}$ inches in breadth, and $\frac{3}{4}$ and $\frac{3}{32}$ inches in thickness, what is its contents in cubic inches? Also, what will its weight be in cast iron, taking the cubical contents of pattern by which to compute the weight, because cast iron contracts in the ratio of $\frac{1}{8}$ of an inch per lineal foot generally?

(See Table of Decimal Equivalents, p. 19.)

$7\frac{1}{8}$ = 7·125
$\frac{3}{4}$ & $\frac{3}{32}$ = ·84375 ×

35625
49875
21375
28500
57000

6·01171875
$15\frac{7}{16}$ inches = 15·4375 ×

3005859375
4208203125
1803515625
2404687500
3005859375
601171875

Contents 92·8059|08203125 in cubic inches.
(See Table, page 22.) ·2622

1856118
1856118
5568354
1856118

24·33370698 weight in lbs. Avoir.

In practical operations such minute computations are not always required, approximations frequently being equally adapted, particularly when time is of consequence; hence, in multiplication of decimals, or of whole numbers and decimals, contracted multiplication is oftentimes had recourse to, the following being the common rule:—

The multiplicand is placed in the usual form; then place the unit figure of the multiplier under that figure of the multiplicand whose place is the last to be retained in the product, and dispose of the rest so that they may all stand in contrary order to that in which they are usually placed. Then, in multiplying, reject all the figures on the right hand of the multiplying digit, and set down each product so that the right hand figures may fall in a vertical line; and observe that the first figure of every line must be increased with what would arise (by carrying 1 from 5 to 14, 2 from 15 to 24, 3 from 25 to 34, 4 from 35 to 44, &c.) from the product of the two preceding figures when you begin to multiply, and the sum is the product required; but the following example, worked out at length, may more advantageously elucidate:—

$7\frac{1}{8} =$	7·125	
$\frac{3}{4}$ & $\frac{3}{32} =$	57348	or ·84375 reversed.
	57000	
	2850	
	214	
	50	
	3	
Product	6·01161	or sectional area in sq. inches.
$15\frac{7}{16} =$	573451	or 15·4375 reversed.
	601171	
	300586	
	24047	
	1803	
	421	
	30	
Product	92·8058	Solidity in cubic inches.
Weight of cubic inch	2262	or ·2622 reversed.
	185612	
	55682	
	1856	
	186	
Product	24·3336	in lbs. Avoirdupois.

Ex. 3. Suppose the above casting is too light, and too long as a counterpoise, it being required 32 lbs. in weight, what length must it be in lead?

Areal section of pattern = 6 inches.
Weight of 1 cubic inch of lead = ·415 lbs.
Then ·415 × 6 = 2·49, and 32 ÷ 2·49 = 12·835 inches in length.

Ounces of dry deal or yellow pine as patterns for castings or forgings, &c.

Multiplied by	1·011 =	lbs.	Avoirdupois	in cast iron.
„ „	1·075 =	„	„	wrought iron.
„ „	1·175 =	„	„	brass.
„ „	1·21 =	„	„	copper.
„ „	1·584 =	„	„	lead.

Ex. Suppose a model or pattern of dry pine equal 3 lbs. 5 ozs. Avoirdupois, what weight will the same be as a forging of wrought iron?

3 lbs. 5 ozs. = 53 ozs. × 1·075 = 56·975 lbs., or 56 lbs. 15 ounces.

Comparative Densities of various Metals.

Bar or Plate Iron being		1·000
Cast Iron...............	=	·942
Steel, soft	=	1·007
„ hard	=	1·016
Brass, cast	=	1·083
Copper, „	=	1·123
„ wrought......	=	1·140
Lead....................	=	1·487

Ex. Required, the weight of 1 lineal foot of round wrought copper to replace 1 lineal foot of round bar iron 1½ inches diameter.

As per table of bar iron, 1 foot of 1½ in. round = 5·92 lbs., and 5·92 × 1·14 = 6·74 lbs. of copper.

Weight of Square and Round Bar Iron in lbs. Avoirdupois.

Inches.	Square.	Round.	Inches.	Square.	Round.
¼	·210	·165	3 inches	30·15	23·68
5/16	·327	·257	3⅛	32·72	25·70
⅜	·471	·370	3¼	35·39	27 80
7/16	·641	·504	3⅜	38·16	29·97
½	·838	·658	3½	41·04	32·23
9/16	1·06	·833	3⅝	44·02	34·58
⅝	1·31	1·03	3¾	47·10	37 00
11/16	1·58	1·25	3⅞	50·25	39·51
¾	1·89	1·48	4 inches	53·60	42·10
13/16	2·21	1·74	4⅛	57·00	44·78
⅞	2·56	2·02	4¼	60·51	47·54
15/16	2·94	2·32	4⅜	64.12	50·17
1 inch	3·35	2·64	4½	67·82	53·28
1⅛	4·24	3·33	4⅝	71·66	56·29
1¼	5·24	4·12	4¾	75·71	59·38
1⅜	6·33	4·98	4⅞	79·60	62·54
1½	7·54	5·92	5 inches	83·75	65·80
1⅝	8·85	6·95	5¼	92·33	72·54
1¾	10·26	8·06	5½	101·33	79·60
1⅞	11·78	9·25	5¾	110·76	87·00
2 inches	13·40	10·53	6 inches	120·60	94·72
2⅛	15·13	11·89	6¼	130·85	102·80
2¼	16·96	13·32	6½	141·56	111·17
2⅜	18 93	14·85	6¾	152·63	119·90
2½	21·00	16·45	7 inches	164·16	129·00
2⅝	23·09	18·14	7½	188·42	148·00
2¾	25·33	19·90	8 inches	214·40	168·40
2⅞	27·69	21·75	9 inches	271·28	213·12

Weights of Round Bar Iron, frequently required for hurried purposes of estimation, &c.

Lengths of the Iron in feet.	Diameters in inches.						
	1 inch	1¼	1½	1¾	2 inches	2¼	2½
	Weights in cwts., qrs., lbs. Avoirdupois.						
1	2·6	4·2	5·9	8·6	10·5	13·3	16·4
2	5·3	8·3	11·8	16·2	21	26·6	1 5
3	7·9	12·4	17·7	24·2	1 4	1 12	1 22
4	10·6	16·5	23·7	1 4	1 14	1 25	2 10
5	13·2	20·6	1 2	1 12	1 25	2 11	2 27
6	15·8	24·7	1 8	1 20	2 8	2 24	3 15
7	18·3	1 1	1 13	2 1	2 18	3 9	1 0 3
8	21·2	1 5	1 20	2 9	3 1	3 23	1 0 20
9	23·8	1 9	1 26	2 17	3 11	1 0 8	1 1 8
10	26·4	1 13	2 3	2 25	3 22	1 0 21	1 1 25
15	1 12	2 6	3 5	1 0 9	1 1 18	1 3 4	2 0 23
20	1 25	2 26	1 0 7	1 1 21	1 3 14	2 1 15	2 3 21
30	2 23	1 0 12	1 2 10	2 0 18	2 3 8	3 2 8	4 1 18
40	3 23	1 1 25	2 0 13	2 3 14	3 3 1	4 3 1	5 3 14
50	1 0 20	1 3 10	2 2 16	3 2 11	4 2 22	5 3 22	7 1 10
60	1 1 18	2 0 23	3 0 20	4 1 8	5 2 16	7 0 16	8 3 7
70	1 2 17	2 2 8	3 2 22	5 0 4	6 2 9	8 1 9	10 1 4
80	1 3 15	2 3 21	4 0 26	5 2 19	7 2 2	9 2 2	11 3 0
90	2 0 14	3 1 6	4 3 1	6 1 25	8 1 24	10 2 23	13 0 25
100	2 1 12	3 2 20	5 1 4	7 0 22	9 1 17	11 3 16	14 2 21

Weights of Flat Bar Iron per lineal foot, in lbs. Avoirdupois.

Breadth in inches.	Thickness in parts of an inch.								
	⅛	3/16	¼	⅜	½	⅝	¾	⅞	1 in.
⅜	·16	·24	·31						
½	·21	·31	·42	·63					
⅝	·26	·39	·52	·78	1·05				
¾	·32	·47	·63	·94	1·26	1·51			
⅞	·37	·55	·73	1·10	1·46	1·83	2·20		
1 in.	·42	·63	·84	1·26	1·68	2·09	2 51	2·93	
1⅛	·47	·70	·94	1·41	1·88	2·36	2·83	3·30	3·77
1¼	·52	·78	1·05	1·57	2 09	2·62	3·14	3·67	4·19
1⅜	·58	·86	1·15	1·73	2·30	2·88	3·45	4·04	4·61
1½	·63	·94	1·26	1·89	2·51	3·14	3·77	4·40	5·03
1⅝	·68	1·02	1·36	2·04	2·72	3·40	4·09	4·77	5.45
1¾	·73	1·10	1·47	2·20	2·93	3·66	4·41	5·13	5 87
1⅞	·78	1·18	1·57	2·36	3·14	3·93	4·71	5·50	6·29
2 in.	·84	1·26	1·68	2·52	3·35	4·19	5·02	5·87	6·70
2¼	·94	1·41	1·88	2·83	3·77	4·71	5·66	6·60	7·54
2½	1·05	1·57	2·09	3·14	4·19	5·23	6·29	7·33	8·40
2¾	1·15	1·73	2·30	3·45	4·61	5·76	6·91	8·07	9·22
3 in.	1·26	1·88	2·51	3·77	5·03	6·28	7·54	8·80	10·05
3¼	1·36	2·04	2·72	4·08	5·44	6·80	8·17	9·53	10·89
3½	1·47	2·20	2·93	4·40	5·86	7·33	8·80	10·26	11·73
3¾	1·57	2·36	3·14	4·71	6·28	7·85	9·43	11·00	12·57
4 in.	1·68	2·51	3·35	5·03	6·70	8·38	10·05	11·73	13·40
4¼	1.78	2·67	3·56	5·34	7·12	8·90	10·68	12·46	14·24
4½	1·89	2·82	3·77	5·65	7·54	9·42	11·31	13·20	15·08
4¾	1·99	2·98	3·97	5·97	7 96	9·95	11·94	13 93.	15·92
5 in.	2·10	3·14	4·19	6·29	8·38	10·47	12.60	14·66	16·75
5½	2·30	3·45	4·60	6·91	9·22	11·52	13·82	16·20	18·43
6 in.	2·52	3·77	5·02	7·54	10·05	12·56	15·08	17·60	20·11

Weight of a superficial foot of Boiler Plate Iron, Sheet Iron, Copper and Brass, in lbs. Avoirdupois.

Thickness in parts of an inch.	Iron.	Thickness by Wire Gauge. No	Iron.	Copper.	Brass.	Thickness by Wire Gauge. No	Iron.	Copper.	Brass.
1/32	1·25	1	12·50	14·50	13·75	16	2·50	2·90	2·75
1/16	2·5	2	12·00	13·90	13 20	17	2·18	2·52	2·40
1/8	5·0	3	11·00	12·75	12·10	18	1·86	2·15	2·04
3/16	7·5	4	10·00	11·60	11·00	19	1·70	1·97	1·87
1/4	10·0	5	8·74	10·10	9·61	20	1·54	1·78	1·69
5/16	12·5	6	8·12	9·40	8 93	21	1·40	1·62	1·54
3/8	15·0	7	7·50	8·70	8·25	22	1·25	1·45	1·37
7/16	17·5	8	6·86	7·90	7·54	23	1·12	1·30	1·23
1/2	20·0	9	6·24	7·20	6·86	24	1·00	1·16	1·10
9/16	22·5	10	5·62	6·50	6·18	25	·90	1·04	·99
5/8	25·0	11	5·00	5.80	5.50	26	·80	·92	·88
11/16	27·5	12	4·38	5·08	4·81	27	·72	·83	·79
3/4	30·0	13	3·75	4·34	4·12	28	·64	·74	·70
7/8	35·0	14	3·12	3·60	3·43	29	·56	·64	·61
1 in.	40·0	15	2·82	3·27	3·10	30	·50	·58	·55

Weight of a lineal foot of Common Angle Iron, for the construction of Steam-boilers, Tanks, &c., in lbs. Avoirdupois.

Breadth, in inches.	Weight, in lbs.	Breadth, in inches.	Weight, in lbs.
3½	14·	2¼	5·
3¼	11·75	2	3·9
3	10·4	1¾	3·3
2¾	8·3	1½	2·7
2½	6·5	1¼	1·8

Weight of a lineal foot of Plain Cast Iron Pipes, without belts or beads, in lbs. Avoirdupois.

Diameter of Bore in inches.	Thickness of Metal in inches.							
ins.	$\frac{3}{8}$	$\frac{1}{2}$	$\frac{5}{8}$	$\frac{3}{4}$	$\frac{7}{8}$	1 inch	$1\frac{1}{8}$	$1\frac{1}{4}$
	lbs.	lbs.	lbs.	lbs.	lbs.	lbs.	lbs.	lbs.
2	8·8	12·4	16·3	20·4				
$2\frac{1}{2}$	10·7	14·9	19·4	24·1				
3	12·5	17·4	22·4	27·8	33·6	39·7	46·0	
$3\frac{1}{2}$	14·4	19·9	25·5	31·5	37·9	44·7	56·6	
4	16·2	22·3	28·6	35·2	42·3	49·6	57·1	65·1
$4\frac{1}{2}$	18·1	24·8	31·7	38·9	46·7	54·6	62·7	71·2
5	20·0	27·3	34·9	42·7	51·0	59·5	68·3	77·4
$5\frac{1}{2}$	21·9	29·8	38·0	46·4	55·3	64·5	73·9	83·4
6	23·7	32·2	41·1	50·1	59·6	69·4	79·4	89·8
$6\frac{1}{2}$	25·6	34·7	44·2	53·8	63·9	74·4	85·0	96·0
7	27·4	37·2	47·3	57·5	68·3	79·3	90·6	102·2
$7\frac{1}{2}$	29·3	39·7	50·4	61·2	72·6	84·3	96·2	108·4
8	31·1	42·2	53·5	65·0	77·0	89·3	101·8	114·6
$8\frac{1}{2}$	33·0	44·7	56·6	68·7	81·3	94·3	107·4	120·8
9	34·9	47·1	59·6	72·4	85·7	99·2	112·9	127·0
$9\frac{1}{2}$	36·8	49·6	62·7	75·6	90·0	104·2	118·5	133·2
10	38·6	52·1	65·8	79·9	94·3	109·1	124·1	139·4
$10\frac{1}{2}$		54·6	68·9	82·8	98·6	114·1	129·7	145·6
11		57·0	72·0	87·3	103·0	119·0	135·2	151·8
$11\frac{1}{2}$		59·6	75·1	90·4	107·3	124·0	140·8	158·0
12		62·0	78·2	94·7	111·7	128·9	146·4	164·2
13			84·4	102·2	120 4	138·8	157·5	176·6
14			90·6	109·6	129·0	148·8	168·7	189·0
15			96·8	117·0	137·7	158·7	179·8	201·4
16				124·5	146·4	168·6	181·0	213·8
17				131·9	155·1	178·5	202·1	224·2
18				138·2	162·1	186·5	211·2	236·2
20					179·3	206·2	233·3	260·8
22						225·8	255·4	285·4
24						245·5	277·3	310·0

NOTE.—Two flanges are generally estimated as equal to

one foot of pipe, but the weights of sockets, belts, and beads are entirely uncertain.

To find the weight of any other diameter of cast iron pipe:—

RULE.—Add together the outside and inside diameters in inches, multiply the sum by their difference and by 2·48, the product is the weight in lbs. Avoirdupois.

Ex. Required the weight of a lineal foot of pipe 30 inches internal diameter, and the metal $1\frac{1}{4}$ inches in thickness.

30 + 2·5 = 32·5 and 32·5 + 30 = 62·5
then 62·5 × 2·5 × 2·48 = 387·5 lbs., or 3 cwt. 1 qr., 23 lbs.

Diameters in inches, and weight in lbs. Avoirdupois, of Cast Iron Balls.

lbs.	inches.	lbs.	inches.		lbs.	inches.
1	$1\frac{7}{8}$ & $\frac{3}{32}$	22	$5\frac{7}{16}$		52	$7\frac{3}{16}$ & $\frac{1}{32}$
2	$2\frac{3}{8}$ & $\frac{3}{32}$	24	$5\frac{9}{16}$		54	$7\frac{5}{16}$ & $\frac{1}{32}$
3	$2\frac{3}{4}$ & $\frac{1}{32}$	26	$5\frac{3}{4}$	$\frac{1}{2}$ cwt.	56	$7\frac{3}{8}$ & $\frac{1}{32}$
4	$3\frac{3}{32}$	28	$5\frac{7}{8}$ & $\frac{1}{32}$		58	$7\frac{1}{2}$
5	$3\frac{5}{16}$	30	$6\frac{1}{32}$		60	$7\frac{1}{2}$ & $\frac{3}{32}$
6	$3\frac{1}{2}$	32	$6\frac{3}{16}$		62	$7\frac{5}{8}$ & $\frac{1}{32}$
7	$3\frac{3}{4}$	34	$6\frac{1}{4}$ & $\frac{1}{32}$		64	$7\frac{3}{4}$
8	$3\frac{7}{8}$	36	$6\frac{3}{8}$ & $\frac{1}{32}$		66	$7\frac{3}{4}$ & $\frac{3}{32}$
9	$4\frac{1}{32}$	38	$6\frac{1}{2}$ & $\frac{1}{32}$		68	$7\frac{7}{8}$ & $\frac{1}{32}$
10	$4\frac{3}{16}$	40	$6\frac{5}{8}$		70	$7\frac{7}{8}$ & $\frac{3}{32}$
12	$4\frac{7}{16}$	42	$6\frac{5}{8}$ & $\frac{3}{32}$	$\frac{3}{4}$ cwt.	84	$8\frac{3}{8}$ & $\frac{3}{32}$
14	$4\frac{11}{16}$	44	$6\frac{13}{16}$	1 cwt.	112	$9\frac{5}{16}$ & $\frac{1}{32}$
16	$4\frac{7}{8}$ & $\frac{1}{32}$	46	$6\frac{14}{16}$	5 ,,	560	$15\frac{7}{8}$ & $\frac{1}{16}$
18	$5\frac{3}{32}$	48	$7\frac{1}{32}$	10 ,,	1120	$20\frac{1}{16}$
20	$5\frac{1}{4}$ & $\frac{1}{32}$	50	$7\frac{1}{8}$ & $\frac{1}{32}$	1 ton.	2240	$25\frac{1}{4}$

Approximate Weights of a cylindrical inch of various Metals, in lbs. Avoirdupois.

Cast Iron	= ·2059	Copper, cast	= ·2462
Bar „	= ·2193	Brass, „	= ·24
Wrought „	= ·2215	Zinc, „	= ·2042
Steel, soft	= ·2207	Tin, „	= ·207
Lead, cast	= ·3259	Mercury at 60° ...	= ·3859

Ex. What will be the weight of a circular plate of cast iron 9 inches diameter and $\frac{3}{4}$ of an inch in thickness?

$$9^2 = 81 \times \cdot 75 = 60 \cdot 75 \times \cdot 2059 = 12 \cdot 5 \text{ lbs.}$$

Table of proportional dimensions for hexagonal nuts and bolt heads, with the number of threads per inch, in accordance with what is commonly called Whitworth's Table.

Diameter of bolts in inches	$\frac{1}{4}$	$\frac{3}{8}$	$\frac{1}{2}$	$\frac{5}{8}$	$\frac{3}{4}$	$\frac{7}{8}$
Threads per inch	20	16	12	11	10	9
Breadth of nuts	$\frac{11}{16}$	$\frac{13}{16}$	1 in.	$1\frac{3}{16}$	$1\frac{3}{8}$	$1\frac{9}{16}$
Breadth over angles	$\frac{13}{16}$	$\frac{15}{16}$	$1\frac{1}{8}$	$1\frac{3}{8}$	$1\frac{5}{8}$	$1\frac{13}{16}$
Thickness of heads & nuts	$\frac{5}{16}$	$\frac{7}{16}$	$\frac{9}{16}$	$\frac{3}{4}$	$\frac{7}{8}$	1 in.
Diameter of bolts in inches	1 in.	$1\frac{1}{8}$	$1\frac{1}{4}$	$1\frac{3}{8}$	$1\frac{1}{2}$	$1\frac{5}{8}$
Threads per inch	8	7	7	6	6	5
Breadth of nuts	$1\frac{3}{4}$	$1\frac{15}{16}$	$2\frac{1}{8}$	$2\frac{5}{16}$	$2\frac{1}{2}$	$2\frac{11}{16}$
Breadth over angles	2 in.	$2\frac{1}{4}$	$2\frac{7}{16}$	$2\frac{11}{16}$	$2\frac{7}{8}$	$3\frac{1}{8}$
Thickness of heads & nuts	$1\frac{1}{8}$	$1\frac{1}{4}$	$1\frac{7}{16}$	$1\frac{9}{16}$	$1\frac{11}{16}$	$1\frac{13}{16}$
Diameter of bolts in inches	$1\frac{3}{4}$	$1\frac{7}{8}$	2 in.	$2\frac{1}{4}$	$2\frac{1}{2}$	3 in.
Threads per inch	5	$4\frac{1}{2}$	$4\frac{1}{2}$	4	4	$3\frac{1}{2}$
Breadth of nuts	$2\frac{7}{8}$	$3\frac{1}{16}$	$3\frac{1}{4}$	$3\frac{5}{8}$	4	—
Breadth over angles	$3\frac{5}{16}$	$3\frac{1}{2}$	$3\frac{3}{4}$	$4\frac{3}{16}$	$4\frac{5}{8}$	—
Thickness of heads & nuts	2 in.	$2\frac{1}{8}$	$2\frac{1}{4}$	$2\frac{1}{2}$	$2\frac{3}{4}$	—

Table exhibiting in successive order various properties of the principal metals.

Malleability.	Ductility.	Tenacity.
Gold	Gold	Wrought Iron
Silver	Silver	Wrt. Copper
Copper	Platinum	Platinum
Tin	Wrought Iron	Silver
Cadmium	Copper	Gold
Platinum	Zinc	Yellow Brass
Lead	Tin	Cast Iron
Zinc	Lead	Zinc
Wrought Iron	Nickel	Tin
Nickel	Palladium	Bismuth
Palladium	Cadmium	Lead

Properties of metals as materials of construction.

Ultimate cohesive strength of an inch square bar in Tons.		Relative strength to resist torsion Lead being 1.	Linear expansion from 32° to 212° Fahr.		Contracts in cooling from fluid to solid state. Parts of an inch per lineal foot.
Cast steel	60	19·5	1 part in	842	·133
Shear do.	57	17·0	,,	890	—
Wrt. iron	25	10·1	,,	812	·137
Gun metal	16	5·0	,,	582	·220
Wrt. copper ...	15	—		—	—
Cast do. ...	$8\frac{1}{2}$	4·3	,,	581	·193
Yellow brass ...	8	4·6	,,	584	·210
Cast iron	$7\frac{3}{4}$	9·0	,,	900	·125
Zinc............ ..	$3\frac{3}{4}$	—	,,	340	·329
Cast tin	2	1·4	,,	462	·278
Bismuth	$1\frac{1}{4}$	—	,,	719	·156
Lead	$\frac{3}{4}$	1·0	,,	351	·319

Melting, boiling, and freezing points of various bodies, in degrees of Fahrenheit.

		Degrees.
Platinum	melts at	3080
Nickel	„	2810
Cast Iron, average	„	2786
Gold, fine	„	2016
Copper	„	1996
Gun Metal	„	1900
Silver, pure	„	1873
Brass	„	1869
Antimony	„	810
Zinc	„	773
Lead	„	594
Bismuth	„	476
Tin 1 and Lead 4	„	460
Tin and Cadmium, each	„	442
Equal parts Tin and Bismuth ...	„	283
Sulphur	„	226
Bismuth 5, Tin 3, and Lead 2 ...	„	214
Bismuth 8, Tin 3, and Lead 5 ...	„	210
Bees-wax	„	151
Spermaceti	„	142
Bismuth 15, Lead 8, Tin 4, and Cadmium 3	„	138
Tallow	„	72
Mercury	boils at	660
Linseed Oil	„	600
Sulphuric Acid	„	590
Oil of Turpentine	„	560
Nitric Acid	„	242
Sea Water	„	213
Fresh Water	„	212
Ditto, in a vacuum	„	98
Olive Oil	freezes at	36
Fresh Water	„	32
Vinegar	„	28
Sea Water	„	27½
Wines, average	„	20
Turpentine	„	14
Sulphuric Acid	„	1

Equal parts Alcohol and Water freezes at 7° below Zero.
Alcohol 2 and Water 1 ... „ 11 „ „
Mercury ... ... „ 39 „ „
Nitric Acid ... ... „ 45½ „ „

NOTE.—Red heat of a common fire equal about 1200° F., and white heat of a smith's forge 2900 F.

Proportions of Metals for the production of useful Alloys.

	Copper.	Tin.	Zinc.
Gun Metal	11	2	0
„	8	1	1
Bronze	4¼	1	0
„	9	1	0
Brass, hard	3¾	1	0
„ sheet	3	0	1
„ yellow	2	0	1
„ deep yellow	1	0	2
Bearings for Machinery	16	2½	½
Muntz's Metal	1½	0	1
Babbit's „ .... and 5 Regulus of Antimony	1	50	
Bell Metal, for large Bells...........	8	2	0
„ „ small „	16	5	0
Spelter Solder for Brass	1	0	1
„ „ „ Copper and Iron	16	0	12
	Lead.		
Tinman's Solder	2	1	0
Plumber's „	1	1	0
Glazier's „	3	1	0

A metal that expands in cooling from the melted state:—Lead 9, Antimony 2, and Bismuth 1.

German Silver :—100 Copper, 60 Zinc, and 40 Nickel.

Mosaic Gold—16 Copper and 16½ Zinc.

Ordinary Type-metal.—15 Lead, 4 Antimony, and 1 Tin.

Britannia Metal:—50 Tin, 4 Antimony, 4 Bismuth, and 1 Copper.

Degrees of temperature necessary to effect the practical color on hardened steel, for the various purposes to which edge tools are applied.

Turning tools for metal	430° Fah.,	very pale straw color.
	to 450	A shade of darker yellow.
Tools for Wood, Screw taps, &c.	470	A dark straw yellow.
	to 490	A dark straw yellow, approximating brown.
Hatchets, chipping chisels, and other percussive tools	500° to 520°	A brown yellow, or yellow slightly tinged with purple.
	530	Light purple.
Springs, &c................	550	Dark purple.
"	570	Dark blue.

Proportionate quantities of Lead and Tin that will when in a melted state produce the various degrees of color on hardened Steel by immersion.

1 lb. of Block Tin to each quantity of clean Lead.

	Degrees.		lbs.	oz.	
Light straw color ...	430	Fah.,	1	14	Lead.
Yellow	450	"	2	2	"
Dark straw yellow...	470	"	2	8	"
Light brown	490	"	3	8	"
Brown yellow	500	"	4	12	"
Light purple	530	"	7	8	"
Dark purple	550	"	12	0	"
Dark blue..............	558	"	25	0	"

Change Wheels for Screw Cutting, the leading Screw of Lathe being ½ inch pitch.

Number of Threads in inch of Screw to be cut.	Number of Teeth in Wheel on Lathe Spindle.	Number of Teeth in Wheel on end of Leading Screw.	A Number of Threads in inch of Screw to be cut.	B Number of Teeth in Wheel on Lathe Spindle.	C Number of Teeth in Wheel in contact with Spindle Wheel.	D Number of Teeth in Pinion in contact with Screw Wheel.	E Number of Teeth in Wheel on end of Leading Screw.
1	80	40	* 8½	90	85	20	90
1¼	80	50	* 9	60	90	20	60
1½	80	60	* 9½	60	60	20	95
1¾	80	70	*10	60	75	20	80
2	60	60	*10½	50	70	20	75
2¼	80	90	*11	60	75	20	80
2½	80	100	*11½	60	115	20	60
2¾	80	110	*12	60	60	20	120
3	80	120	13	20	65	60	120
3¼	80	130	14	20	70	60	120
3¼	40	65	15	20	75	60	120
3½	80	140	16	20	80	60	120
3½	40	70	17	20	85	60	120
3¾	80	150	18	20	90	60	120
3¾	40	75	19	20	95	60	120
4	40	80	20	20	100	60	120
4¼	40	85	21	20	105	60	120
4½	40	90	22	20	110	60	120
4¾	40	95	23	20	115	60	120
5	40	100	24	65	120	20	130
5½	40	110	24	55	120	20	110
6	40	120	25	60	100	20	150
6½	40	130	25	30	100	20	75
6½	20	65	26	70	130	20	140
7	40	140	26	20	120	30	65
7	20	70	28	75	140	20	150
7½	40	150	30	70	140	20	150
7½	20	75	32	30	80	20	120
8	30	120	34	30	85	20	120
8½	20	85	36	30	90	20	120
9	20	90	38	30	95	20	120
9½	20	95	40	30	100	20	120
10	20	100	42	30	105	20	120
10½	20	105	44	30	110	20	120
11	20	110	46	30	115	20	120
11½	20	115	48	25	120	20	100
12	20	120	50	30	100	20	150

The Pitches in the preceding Table marked * are repeated for the convenience of those who may prefer using the compound series.

NOTE.—If the Leading Screw coutains four threads to the inch ($\frac{1}{4}$ inch pitch), the screw to be cut will have double the number of threads given in the foregoing Table.

To calculate for the Change Wheels when any other pitch of leading screw is given or required—

Let A represent the number of threads to be cut per inch;

B, the number of teeth in wheel on lathe spindle;

C, the number of teeth in wheel in contact with spindle wheel;

D, the number of teeth in wheel in contact with leading screw wheel;

E, the number of teeth in wheel on end of leading screw; and

n, the pitch of leading screw per inch.

Then, $$\frac{A \times B \times D}{E \times n} = C.$$

$$\frac{A \times B \times C}{E \times n} = D.$$

$$\frac{C \times E \times n}{A \times D} = B.$$

$$\frac{A \times B \times D}{C \times n} = E.$$

Arithmetically thus:—

Let the leading screw equal $\frac{1}{2}$ inch pitch, or 2 threads per inch, and the screw to be cut $10\frac{1}{2}$ threads per inch.

Take any 3 of the screw cutting wheels that can be conveniently applied, say B of 50 teeth, E of 75, and D of 20, to find the number of teeth required in C.

$$\frac{10{\cdot}5 \times 50 \times 20}{75 \times 2} = \frac{10500}{150} = 70 \text{ teeth in C.}$$

To determine the number of teeth or pitch of small wheels, on the Manchester principle.

In this mode of finding the number of teeth for any wheel of a given diameter, or the diameter of a pitch circle to contain any required number of teeth, simplicity is the chief aim, by evasion of fractional parts in the calculation. To effect this, the division of the pitch circle is entirely disregarded, and the pitch or number of teeth is determined by whole numbers on the pitch circle's diameter, and called the diametral pitch, whereby to distinguish between that and the common or circular pitch. In the following table the circular pitches are merely notified, so as to give some idea of the size of the teeth, by which to select what might be best adapted in strength to any particular purpose required.

Table of Pitches.

Diametral pitch.	Circular pitch in decimals.	Circular pitch in fractions.	Diametral pitch.	Circular pitch in decimals.	Circular pitch in fractions.
3	1·047	1 & $\frac{1}{32}$ ins.	9	·349	$\frac{1}{4}$ & $\frac{3}{32}$
4	·785	$\frac{3}{4}$ & $\frac{1}{32}$	10	·314	$\frac{1}{4}$ & $\frac{1}{16}$
5	·628	$\frac{5}{8}$	12	·262	$\frac{1}{4}$
6	·524	$\frac{1}{2}$ inch	14	·224	$\frac{1}{8}$ & $\frac{3}{32}$
7	·449	$\frac{3}{8}$ & $\frac{1}{16}$	16	·196	$\frac{1}{8}$ & $\frac{1}{16}$
8	·393	$\frac{3}{8}$	20	·157	$\frac{1}{8}$ & $\frac{1}{32}$

1. To find what number of teeth any wheel of a given diameter of pitch circle will contain, or divide into, of a required pitch :—

Rule.—Multiply the diameter of the pitch circle in inches by the given diametral pitch, and the product is the number of teeth.

Ex. Required the number of teeth in a wheel of 15 inches, and of 6 pitch.

$$15 \times 6 = 90 \text{ teeth of } \tfrac{1}{2} \text{ inch circular pitch.}$$

2. To determine the diameter of pitch circle to contain a given number of teeth of a given pitch:—

RULE.—Divide the given number of teeth by the required diametral pitch, and the quotient is the diameter of pitch circle.

Ex. What diameter of pitch circle is necessary for a wheel of 172 teeth and of 16 pitch?

$172 \div 16 = 10{\cdot}75$ inches,—circular pitch $= \frac{3}{16}$ of an inch.

Table of approximate numbers by which to determine the diameter of any pitch circle for a toothed wheel when the pitch of teeth and number are given; also, to find what number of teeth of a given pitch any given diameter of pitch circle will divide into.

Pitch in inches.	To find the diameter.	To find the number of teeth.	Pitch in inches.	To find the diameter.	To find the number of teeth.
$\frac{1}{2}$	·1592	6·2832	2 ins.	·6366	1·5708
$\frac{5}{8}$	·1989	5·0266	$2\frac{1}{8}$	·6764	1·4773
$\frac{3}{4}$	·2387	4·1888	$2\frac{1}{4}$	·7135	1·3963
$\frac{7}{8}$	·2785	3·5901	$2\frac{3}{8}$	·7560	1·3240
1 inch	·3183	3·1416	$2\frac{1}{2}$	·7958	1·2566
$1\frac{1}{8}$	·3568	2·7926	$2\frac{3}{4}$	·8754	1·1333
$1\frac{1}{4}$	·3979	2·5132	3 ins.	·9547	1·0472
$1\frac{3}{8}$	·4377	2·2848	$3\frac{1}{4}$	1·0345	·9667
$1\frac{1}{2}$	·4774	2·0944	$3\frac{1}{2}$	1·1141	·8976
$1\frac{5}{8}$	·5141	1·9264	4	1·2732	·7854
$1\frac{3}{4}$	·5370	1·7952	5	1·5915	·6283
$1\frac{7}{8}$	·5937	1·6755	6	1·9095	·5236

Rule 1.—Multiply the numbers corresponding to the pitch in the columns 2 or 5, and the product is the diameter of pitch circle in inches.

Ex. Suppose a wheel of 128 teeth is required of $2\frac{1}{8}$ pitch.

$\cdot 6764 \times 128 = 86\cdot5792$ or $86\frac{1}{2}$ and $\frac{1}{16}$ inches the diameter.

Rule 2.—Multiply the numbers corresponding to the pitch in columns 3 or 6, and the product will show the number, plus or minus, that the circle will divide into at the given pitch.

Ex. A pitch circle is required to be divided into $1\frac{1}{2}$ inch pitch, the diameter is $43\frac{1}{2}$ inches; what will be the number of teeth?

$2\cdot0944 \times 43\cdot5 = 91\cdot1$ teeth, hence the circle is plus $\frac{1}{10}$th of the pitch towards another tooth.

The diameter of pitch circle being given, and also the number of teeth required,—To find the pitch into which it will divide.

Rule.—Multiply 3·1416 by the circle's diameter in inches, and divide the product by the number of teeth; the quotient is the pitch in inches.

Thus, suppose a pitch circle of $43\frac{1}{2}$ inches to be divided into 91 teeth, what will be the pitch?

$$3\cdot1416 \times 43\cdot5 = \frac{136\cdot6596}{91} = 1\cdot501 \text{ inches, and}$$

such measurements can only be obtained from the decimal scale of inches, as annexed in the work.

Pitch of the Teeth of Wheels proportionate in strength to a given amount of Horses' Power nominally, at various velocities.

Pitch	Thickness	Breadth	Velocities at the Pitch Circles, in feet per minute, viz.,			
			180	240	300	420
of Teeth in inches.			Horses' Power.			
4	1·9	8	19	25·5	32	45
3½	1·6	7	14·75	19·5	24·5	34·25
3	1·4	6	11	14·5	18	25
2½	1·2	5	7·5	10	12·5	17·5
2	·95	4	4·75	6·25	8	11
1¾	·83	3·5	3·5	5	6·25	6·25
1½	·71	3	2·75	3·5	4·5	4·5
1¼	·59	2·5	2	2·5	3·125	3·5
1⅛	·53	2·25	1·5	2·25	2·5	2·8
1 inch	·48	2	1·2	1·6	2	2·5

Restrictions relative to Wheels and Pinions in working contact, that ought to be attended to.

1. When wheels drive pinions, let no pinion have less than 8 teeth, rather 11 or 12 if possibly convenient.

2. When pinions drive wheels, let no pinion have less than 6 teeth, rather 8 or 9.

3. The number of teeth in a wheel should be prime to the number of teeth in a pinion: that is, suppose a pinion to contain 9 teeth, and required to make 6 revolutions for 1 of the wheel; 6 times 9 = 54 teeth, and one added = 55 teeth in the wheel.

4. To increase or diminish velocity in a given proportion, and with the least quantity of wheel work, let the number of teeth on each pinion be to the number of teeth on its wheel as 1 to 6; that is, never let more than 6 teeth be in the wheel for 1 in the pinion.

Number of Teeth.	Pitch of the Teeth in inches.								
	½	⅝	¾	⅞	1 in.	1⅛	1¼	1⅜	1½
	Diameter of Pitch Circle in feet and inches.								
96	1 3¼	1 7	1 10⅞	2 2¾	2 6½	2 10⅜	3 2⅛	3 6	3 9¾
97	1 3⅜	1 7¼	1 11⅛	2 3	2 6⅞	2 10¾	3 2⅝	3 6½	3 10¼
98	1 3½	1 7½	1 11⅜	2 3¼	2 7⅛	2 11	3 3	3 6⅞	3 10¾
99	1 3¾	1 7⅝	1 11⅝	2 3⅝	2 7½	2 11⅜	3 3⅜	3 7⅜	3 11¼
100	1 3⅞	1 7⅞	1 11⅞	2 3¾	2 7⅞	2 11⅞	3 3¾	3 7¾	3 11¾
101	1 4	1 8	2 0⅛	2 4⅛	2 8¼	3 0⅛	3 4⅛	3 8¼	4 0¼
102	1 4¼	1 8¼	2 0¼	2 4⅜	2 8½	3 0½	3 4½	3 8⅝	4 0⅝
103	1 4⅜	1 8½	2 0½	2 4⅝	2 8¾	3 0¾	3 4⅞	3 9	4 1⅛
104	1 4½	1 8⅝	2 0¾	2 4⅞	2 9⅛	3 1⅛	3 5⅜	3 9½	4 1⅝
105	1 4¾	1 8⅞	2 1	2 5¼	2 9½	3 1½	3 5¾	3 9⅞	4 2⅛
106	1 4⅞	1 9	2 1¼	2 5½	2 9¾	3 1⅞	3 6⅛	3 10¼	4 2⅝
107	1 5	1 9¼	2 1½	2 5¾	2 10⅛	3 2⅛	3 6½	3 10⅞	4 3
108	1 5⅛	1 9½	2 1¾	2 6	2 10⅜	3 2½	3 6⅞	3 11¼	4 3½
109	1 5¼	1 9⅝	2 2	2 6⅜	2 10⅝	3 2⅞	3 7⅜	3 11¾	4 4
110	1 5½	1 9⅞	2 2¼	2 6⅝	2 11	3 3¼	3 7¾	4 0⅛	4 4½
111	1 5⅝	1 10	2 2½	2 6⅞	2 11¼	3 3½	3 8⅛	4 0½	4 5
112	1 5¾	1 10¼	2 2¾	2 7⅛	2 11⅝	3 3⅞	3 8½	4 1	4 5½
113	1 5⅞	1 10½	2 3	2 7½	2 11⅞	3 4¼	3 8⅞	4 1½	4 6
114	1 6⅛	1 10⅝	2 3¼	2 7¾	3 0¼	3 4⅝	3 9⅜	4 1⅞	4 6½
115	1 6¼	1 10⅞	2 3½	2 8	3 0⅝	3 5	3 9¾	4 2¼	4 7
116	1 6⅜	1 11	2 3⅝	2 8¼	3 0⅞	3 5⅜	3 10⅛	4 2¾	4 7⅜
117	1 6⅝	1 11¼	2 3⅞	2 8½	3 1¼	3 5¾	3 10½	4 3¼	4 7⅞
118	1 6¾	1 11½	2 4⅛	2 8⅞	3 1½	3 6⅛	3 10⅞	4 3⅝	4 8¼
119	1 6⅞	1 11⅝	2 4⅜	2 9⅛	3 1⅞	3 6½	3 11⅜	4 4	4 8¾
120	1 7⅛	1 11⅞	2 4⅝	2 9½	3 2¼	3 6⅞	3 11¾	4 4½	4 9¼
121	1 7¼	2 0	2 4⅞	2 9¾	3 2½	3 7⅛	4 0⅛	4 5	4 9¾
122	1 7⅜	2 0¼	2 5⅛	2 9⅞	3 2⅞	3 7½	4 0½	4 5⅜	4 10¼
123	1 7½	2 0½	2 5¼	2 10¼	3 3⅛	3 7⅞	4 0⅞	4 5⅞	4 10¾
124	1 7¾	2 0⅝	2 5½	2 10½	3 3½	3 8¼	4 1¼	4 6¼	4 11⅛
125	1 7⅞	2 0⅞	2 5⅞	2 10¾	3 3¾	3 8½	4 1¾	4 6¾	4 11⅝

Number of Teeth.	Pitch of the Teeth in inches.								
	1⅝	1¾	1⅞	2 in.	2⅛	2¼	2½	2¾	3 in.
	Diameter of Pitch Circle in feet and inches.								
126	5 4¾	5 10⅛	6 2¾	6 8¼	7 1¼	7 6	8 4¼	9 2¼	10 0¼
127	5 5¼	5 10¾	6 3⅜	6 8¾	7 2	7 6⅝	8 5	9 3⅛	10 1¼
128	5 5⅞	5 11¼	6 4	6 9½	7 2½	7 7¼	8 5⅞	9 4	10 2¼
129	5 6⅜	5 11⅞	6 4⅝	6 10⅛	7 3¼	7 8	8 6⅝	9 4⅞	10 3⅛
130	5 6⅞	6 0⅜	6 5⅛	6 10¾	7 4	7 8¾	8 7½	9 5¾	10 4⅛
131	5 7⅜	6 1	6 5¾	6 11⅜	7 4¾	7 9½	8 8¼	9 6⅝	10 5
132	5 7⅞	6 1½	6 6⅜	7 0	7 5⅜	7 10⅛	8 9	9 7½	10 6
133	5 8⅜	6 2	6 7	7 0⅝	7 6	7 10⅞	8 9¾	9 8⅜	10 7
134	5 8⅞	6 2⅝	6 7½	7 1¼	7 6⅝	7 11½	8 10⅝	9 9¼	10 8
135	5 9½	6 3⅛	6 8⅛	7 2	7 7¼	8 0¼	8 11⅜	9 10⅛	10 8⅞
136	5 10	6 3¾	6 8¾	7 2⅝	7 8	8 1	9 0¼	9 11	10 9¾
137	5 10½	6 4¼	6 9¼	7 3¼	7 8⅝	8 1¾	9 1	10 0	10 10¾
138	5 11	6 4¾	6 10	7 3¾	7 9¼	8 2½	9 1¾	10 0⅞	10 11¾
139	5 11½	6 5½	6 10½	7 4⅜	7 10	8 3⅛	9 2⅝	10 1⅝	11 0⅝
140	6 0	6 6	6 11⅛	7 5⅛	7 10⅝	8 3⅞	9 3⅜	10 2½	11 1⅝
141	6 0½	6 6½	6 11¾	7 5¾	7 11⅜	8 4½	9 4¼	10 3⅜	11 2½
142	6 1	6 7	7 0¼	7 6¾	8 0	8 5¼	9 5	10 4¼	11 3½
143	6 1½	6 7⅝	7 0⅞	7 7	8 0¾	8 6	9 5¾	10 5⅛	11 4½
144	6 2	6 8¼	7 1½	7 7⅝	8 1⅜	8 6¾	9 6;	10 6	11 5½
145	6 2½	6 8¾	7 2	7 8¼	8 2	8 7½	9 7⅜	10 6⅞	11 6½
146	6 3	6 9¼	7 2⅝	7 9	8 2¾	8 8⅛	9 8⅛	10 7¾	11 7⅜
147	6 3½	6 9⅞	7 3¼	7 9½	8 3⅜	8 8⅞	9 9	10 8⅝	11 8¼
148	6 4	6 10½	7 3⅞	7 10¼	8 4⅛	8 9⅝	9 9¾	10 9½	11 9¼
149	6 4½	6 11	7 4½	7 10¾	8 4⅞	8 10¼	9 10½	10 10⅜	11 10¼
150	6 5⅛	6 11½	7 5	7 11½	8 5½	8 11	9 11⅜	10 11¼	11 11¼

Number of Teeth.	Pitch of the Teeth in inches.								
	½	⅝	¾	⅞	1 in.	1⅛	1¼	1⅜	1½
	Diameter of Pitch Circle in feet and inches.								
126	1 8	2 1	2 6	2 11	3 4⅛	3 8⅞	4 2⅛	4 7⅛	5 0⅛
127	1 8⅛	2 1¼	2 6¼	2 11⅜	3 4½	3 9¼	4 2½	4 7½	5 0⅝
128	1 8⅜	2 1⅜	2 6½	2 11⅝	3 4¾	3 9⅝	4 2⅞	4 8	5 1⅛
129	1 8½	2 1⅝	2 6¾	2 11⅞	3 5	3 10	4 3¼	4 8½	5 1½
130	1 8⅝	2 1⅞	2 7	3 0¼	3 5⅜	3 10⅜	4 3¾	4 9	5 2
131	1 8¾	2 2	2 7¼	3 0½	3 5⅝	3 10¾	4 4⅛	4 9⅜	5 2½
132	1 9	2 2¼	2 7½	3 0¾	3 6	3 11	4 4½	4 9¾	5 3
133	1 9⅛	2 2½	2 7¾	3 1	3 6¼	3 11½	4 4⅞	4 10¼	5 3½
134	1 9¼	2 2⅝	2 7⅞	3 1¼	3 6⅝	3 11⅞	4 5¼	4 10⅝	5 4
135	1 9½	2 2⅞	2 8¼	3 1½	3 6⅞	4 0⅛	4 5¾	4 11	5 4½
136	1 9⅝	2 3	2 8½	3 1⅞	3 7¼	4 0½	4 6⅛	4 11½	5 5
137	1 9¾	2 3¼	2 8¾	3 2⅛	3 7½	4 0⅞	4 6½	5 0	5 5⅜
138	1 9⅞	2 3½	2 9	3 2⅜	3 7⅞	4 1¼	4 6⅞	5 0⅜	5 5⅞
139	1 10⅛	2 3⅝	2 9⅛	3 2¾	3 8¼	4 1½	4 7¼	5 0⅞	5 6¼
140	1 10¼	2 3⅞	2 9⅜	3 3	3 8½	4 1⅞	4 7¾	5 1¼	5 6¾
141	1 10½	2 4	2 9⅝	3 3¼	3 8⅞	4 2¼	4 8⅛	5 1¾	5 7¼
142	1 10⅝	2 4¼	2 9⅞	3 3½	3 9⅛	4 2⅝	4 8½	5 2⅛	5 7¾
143	1 10¾	2 4½	2 10⅛	3 3⅞	3 9½	4 3	4 8⅞	5 2½	5 8¼
144	1 10⅞	2 4⅝	2 10⅜	3 4⅛	3 9¾	4 3⅜	4 9¼	5 3	5 8¾
145	1 11	2 4⅞	2 10⅝	3 4⅜	3 10⅛	4 3¾	4 9⅝	5 3½	5 9¼
146	1 11¼	2 5	2 10¾	3 4⅝	3 10½	4 4	4 10	5 4	5 9¾
147	1 11⅜	2 5¼	2 11	3 4⅞	3 10¾	4 4½	4 10½	5 4⅜	5 10⅛
148	1 11⅝	2 5½	2 11¼	3 5¼	3 11⅛	4 4⅞	4 10⅞	5 4¾	5 10⅝
149	1 11¾	2 5⅝	2 11½	3 5½	3 11½	4 5⅛	4 11¼	5 5¼	5 11⅛
150	1 11⅞	2 5⅞	2 11¾	3 5¾	3 11¾	4 5½	4 11⅝	5 5⅝	5 11⅝

Number of Teeth.	Pitch of the Teeth in inches.								
	1⅝	1¾	1⅞	2 in.	2⅛	2¼	2½	2¾	3 in.
	Diameter of Pitch Circle in feet and inches.								
126	5 4¾	5 10⅛	6 2¾	6 8¼	7 1¼	7 6	8 4¼	9 2¼	10 0¼
127	5 5¼	5 10¾	6 3⅜	6 8¾	7 2	7 6⅝	8 5	9 3⅛	10 1¼
128	5 5⅞	5 11¼	6 4	6 9½	7 2½	7 7¼	8 5⅞	9 4	10 2¼
129	5 6⅜	5 11⅞	6 4⅛	6 10⅛	7 3¼	7 8	8 6⅝	9 4⅞	10 3⅛
130	5 6⅞	6 0⅜	6 5⅛	6 10¾	7 4	7 8¾	8 7½	9 5¾	10 4⅛
131	5 7⅜	6 1	6 5¾	6 11⅜	7 4½	7 9⅛	8 8¼	9 6⅝	10 5
132	5 7⅞	6 1½	6 6⅜	7 0	7 5⅛	7 10⅛	8 9	9 7⅛	10 6
133	5 8⅜	6 2	6 7	7 0⅝	7 6	7 10⅞	8 9¾	9 8⅜	10 7
134	5 8⅞	6 2⅝	6 7½	7 1¼	7 6⅝	7 11½	8 10⅝	9 9¼	10 8
135	5 9½	6 3⅛	6 8⅛	7 2	7 7¼	8 0¼	8 11⅜	9 10⅛	10 8⅞
136	5 10	6 3¾	6 8¾	7 2⅜	7 8	8 1	9 0¼	9 11	10 9¾
137	5 10½	6 4¼	6 9¼	7 3¼	7 8⅝	8 1¾	9 1	10 0	10 10¾
138	5 11	6 4¾	6 10	7 3¾	7 9¼	8 2⅜	9 1¾	10 0⅞	10 11¾
139	5 11½	6 5½	6 10½	7 4⅜	7 10	8 3⅛	9 2⅝	10 1⅝	11 0⅝
140	6 0	6 6	6 11⅛	7 5⅛	7 10⅝	8 3⅞	9 3⅜	10 2½	11 1⅝
141	6 0½	6 6½	6 11¾	7 5¾	7 11⅜	8 4½	9 4¼	10 3⅜	11 2½
142	6 1	6 7	7 0⅜	7 6¾	8 0	8 5¼	9 5	10 4¼	11 3⅜
143	6 1½	6 7⅝	7 0⅞	7 7	8 0¾	8 6	9 5¾	10 5⅛	11 4½
144	6 2	6 8¼	7 1½	7 7⅝	8 1⅜	8 6¾	9 6	10 6	11 5⅜
145	6 2½	6 8¾	7 2	7 8¼	8 2	8 7½	9 7⅜	10 6⅞	11 6½
146	6 3	6 9¼	7 2⅝	7 9	8 2¾	8 8⅛	9 8⅛	10 7¾	11 7⅜
147	6 3½	6 9⅞	7 3¼	7 9½	8 3⅜	8 3⅞	9 9	10 8⅝	11 8¼
148	6 4	6 10½	7 3⅞	7 10¼	8 4⅛	8 9⅝	9 9¾	10 9½	11 9¼
149	6 4½	6 11	7 4½	7 10¾	8 4⅞	8 10¼	9 10⅛	10 10⅜	11 10¼
150	6 5⅛	6 11½	7 5	7 11½	8 5½	8 11	9 11⅜	10 11¼	11 11¼

number 459, divide the greater sum by the lesser, multiply the quotient by the volume at the lower temperature, and the product is the expanded volume in equal terms of unity.

Ex. If the volume of steam produced from water at 212° Fahrenheit equal 1711 times the bulk of the water from which it is produced, what will be the expanded volume at 250·3°, supposing the pressure to be the same in both cases?

$$\frac{250{\cdot}3 + 459}{212 + 459} = \frac{709{\cdot}3}{671} \times 1711 = 1808{\cdot}66$$

To find the elastic force of steam at any given temperature:—

Rule.—To the indicated temperature of the steam in degrees of Fahrenheit add 100, multiply the sum by ·00564, and the sixth power of the product equal the force in inches of mercury, which being multiplied by ·491, equal lbs. per square inch elastic force.

Ex. Suppose steam at a temperature of 262° Fahrenheit.

$262° + 100 \times {\cdot}00564 = 2{\cdot}041686^6 = 74$ inches of mercury, and $74 \times {\cdot}491 = 36{\cdot}3$ lbs. elastic force.

Steam possesses the property of expansive force, and in the following ratio, viz.: If expanded to double its volume of formation, its retaining force equals one-half, if to three times its volume, one-third, if to four times its volume, one-fourth, &c., in an inverse ratio with the degree of expansion; hence the beneficial properties of high-pressure steam in preference to low pressure in the economical working of a steam engine, if cut off early in the stroke, and continued to the end by expansive force. Thus, let dense steam be stopped off from the cylinder of an engine at one-half the stroke, the mean elastic force of the steam throughout the whole stroke equal 1·7; that is, the dense steam equal 1,—and the same steam expanded, terminate at half the original density, but by its increase of volume and diminution of elastic force, seven-tenths of the original elastic force is economised by the property of its expansion; and similar values are obtained in similar ratios when stopped off at any other point of the stroke, as in the following table:—

	½		1·7	
	⅓	of the stroke, the	2·1	of mean elastic
Steam	¼	uniform elastic	2·4	force throughout
stopped	⅕	force by density	2·6	the whole stroke
off at	⅙	and expansion	2·8	in terms of initial
	⅐	equal	3·0	density.
	⅛		3·2	

To determine where steam of any given density must be cut off, so as to retain a certain amount of elastic force at the end, or any other required point of the stroke.

Rule.—Multiply the required elastic force of the steam at the given point or termination of the stroke, as it may be, and divide the product by the given force of the dense steam; the quotient is the distance from commencement of the stroke at which the dense steam must be cut off.

Ex. Suppose steam at 20 lbs, per square inch, length of stroke 24 inches, and at the termination of the stroke the steam to have an elastic force of 7 lbs. per square inch.

$\frac{7 \times 24}{20} = 8{\cdot}4$ inches from the commencement of the stroke.

Salt or sea water does not boil at an equal temperature with that of fresh water, consequently it is an inferior medium of calorific reception for the production of steam, and as the water becomes evaporated, so is saturation approximated and a higher temperature required to produce steam of equal density to that from fresh water.

Sea water naturally holds in solution about $\frac{1}{33}$rd its weight of salt, which becomes more and more augmented by evaporation, each grade as approaching to saturation requiring a higher degree of temperature in attaining the boiling point; thus, sea water in its natural state boils at 213·2° Fahrenheit; at $\frac{2}{33}$rds of saturation the boiling point is 214·4°; at $\frac{3}{33}$rds it is 215·5°; and at $\frac{4}{33}$rds the boiling point is elevated to 216·7°: and which grade of saturation the water in any sea-going vessel's boilers ought never to be allowed to exceed.

Elastic force of steam, and corresponding temperature of the water with which it is in contact.

Pressure of steam per square inch, as indicated by steam pressure gauge, or safety valve. lbs. Avs.	Temperature in degrees of			Volume of steam compared with volume of water.	Cubic inches of water in a cubic foot of steam.
	Fahrenheit.	Reaumur.	Centigrade		
1	216·3	81·9	102·4	1573	1·099
2	219·6	83·3	104·2	1488	1·162
3	222·7	84.7	105·9	1411	1·226
4	225·6	86·0	107·6	1343	1·287
5	228·5	87·3	109·2	1281	1·350
6	231·2	88·5	110·7	1225	1·411
7	233·8	89·7	112·1	1174	1·474
8	236·3	90·8	113·5	1127	1·536
9	238·7	91·9	114·8	1084	1·597
10	241·0	93·0	116·1	1044	1·658
11	243·3	93·9	117·4	1007	1·719
12	245·5	94·9	118·6	973	1·779
13	247·6	95·8	119·8	941	1·840
14	249·6	96·7	120·9	911	1·910
15	251·6	97·6	122·0	883	1·959
16	253·6	98·5	123·1	857	2·021
17	255·5	99·3	124·2	833	2·079
18	257·3	100·1	125·2	810	2·138
19	259·1	100·9	126·2	788	2·198
20	260·9	101·7	127·2	767	2·258
21	262·6	102·5	128·1	748	2·316
22	264·3	103·2	129·1	729	2·376
23	265·9	104·0	129·9	712	2·433
24	267·5	104·7	130·8	695	2·493
25	269·1	105·4	131·7	679	2·552
26	270·6	106·0	132·6	664	2·610
27	272·1	106·7	133·4	649	2·670
28	273·6	107·4	134·2	635	2·725
29	275·0	108·0	135·0	622	2·787
30	276·4	108·6	135·8	610	2·842

Pressure of steam per square inch, as indicated by steam pressure guage, or safety valve.

lbs. Avs.	Temperature in degrees of			Volume of steam compared with volume of water.	Cubic inches of water in a cubic foot of steam.
.	Fahrenheit.	Reaumur.	Centigrade		
31	277·8	109·2	136·6	598	2·899
32	279·2	109·9	137·3	586	2·958
33	280·5	110·4	138·1	575	3·015
34	281·9	111·1	138·8	564	3·074
35	283·2	111·6	139·6	554	3·130
36	284·4	112·2	140·2	544	3·188
37	285·7	112·8	140·9	534	3·248
38	286·9	113·3	141·6	525	3·304
39	288·1	113·8	142·3	516	3·361
40	289·3	114·4	142·9	508	3·415
41	290·5	114·9	143·6	500	3·562
42	291·7	115·4	144·3	492	3·469
43	292·9	116·0	144·9	484	3·526
44	294·2	116·5	145·7	477	3·585
45	295·6	117·2	146·4	470	3·700
46	296·9	117·7	147·2	463	3·756
47	298·1	118·3	147·8	456	3·814
48	299·2	118·8	148·4	449	3·865
49	300·3	119·2	149·1	443	3·927
50	301·3	119·7	149·6	437	3·981
51	302·4	120·2	150·2	431	4·037
52	303·4	120·6	150·8	425	4·094
53	304·4	121·1	151·3	419	4·143
54	305·4	121·5	151·9	414	4·204
55	306·4	122·0	152·4	408	4·256
56	307·4	122·4	153·0	403	4·309
57	308·4	122·8	153·6	398	4·363
58	309·3	123·2	154·1	393	4·419
59	310·3	123·7	154·6	388	4·476
60	311·2	124·1	155·1	383	4·535
61	312·2	124·5	155·7	379	4·583
62	313·1	124·9	156·2	374	4·645
63	314·0	125·3	156·7	370	4·695

Pressure of steam per square inch, as indicated by steam pressure gauge, or safety valve. lbs. Avs.	Temperature in degrees of Fahrenheit.	Reaumur.	Centigrade	Volume of steam compared with volume of water.	Cubic inches of water in a cubic foot of steam.
64	314·9	125·7	157·2	366	4·747
65	315·8	126·1	157·7	362	4·812
66	316·7	126·5	158·2	358	4·826
67	317·6	126·9	158·7	354	4·881
68	318·4	127·3	159·1	350	4·937
69	319·3	127·7	159·6	346	4·994
70	320·1	128·0	160·1	342	5·052
71	321·0	128·4	160·6	339	5·097
72	321·8	128·8	161·0	335	5·158
73	322·6	129·2	161·4	332	5·205
74	323·5	129·6	161·9	328	5·268
75	324·3	129·9	162·4	325	5·317
76	325·1	130·3	162·8	322	5·366
77	325·9	130·6	163·3	319	5·416
78	326·7	131·0	163·7	316	5·468
79	327·5	131·3	164·2	313	5·521
80	328·2	131·6	164·8	310	5·574

NOTE.—In the application of any of the above indicated pressures of steam to a condensing engine, 15 lbs., or one atmosphere, must be added, because the effective pressure in a condensing engine is the indicated pressure plus the atmospheric pressure, minus the resisting vapour remaining in the condenser, as shown by any indicator diagram taken from the cylinder, by which to test the merits or demerits of the engine in regard to useful effect.

Thus, suppose an indicated pressure of 18 lbs. per square inch is applied to a condensing engine,—$18 + 15 = 33$ lbs. as initial density, but the diagram taken shows existing vapour in the condenser, or other defects equal to $5\frac{1}{2}$ lbs.; consequently, $33 - 5\frac{1}{2} = 27\frac{1}{2}$ lbs. per square inch of effective force upon the piston's area.

The steam engine is rendered an available source of motive power through the following innate properties of steam, viz.:—elastic force, expansive force, and ready submission to the destruction of its aeriform state through the abstraction of its heat by cold water, thus constituting the principles of the condensing engine.

In engines on the non-condensing principle condensation of the steam is evaded by excess of density, and after having performed its duty in the cylinder, is allowed to escape into the atmosphere; hence, the atmospheric pressure on the boiler is a counterpoise to the effluent steam from the cylinder, minus its resistance by velocity against the pressure of the atmosphere.

Steam, as regards its various theoretical vicissitudes of beneficial effect in the steam engine, has long been investigated and experimented upon by eminent engineers, and the results of their researches and experiments have been given as data by which to construct upon, both relative to economy and design of modification, suitable to the numerous useful purposes to which the steam engine is applied.

In the constructing and working of stationary engines, it is necessary to be guided by some restricted velocity for the piston in a given time (*say feet per minute*), whereby to effect a maximum of power from a given pressure of steam necessary to the required performance of machinery, &c., at a steady uniform rate of motion; but engines for marine purposes, or for locomotive purposes, have no restricted velocities to contend with, otherwise than economising of fuel and unavoidable want of steam occasionally.

Several empirical rules have been, and still are, in use, whereby to determine the most advantageous velocities for the pistons of steam engines, through which to obtain a maximum of useful effect; but, having found them so contradictory, I have abandoned the idea of any rule in that respect, and substituted the following table, being from the practice of eminent engineers, and combined with my own practical observations, as strictly attended to.

Table of Velocities for the Pistons of Stationary Engines, with given lengths of stroke.

Condensing Engines.			Non-Condensing Engines.		
Length in feet and inches.	Number per minute.	Velocity in feet per minute.	Length in feet and inches.	Number per minute.	Velocity in feet per minute.
2 0	42	168	0 9	100	150
2 3	38	171	1 0	80	160
2 6	35	175	1 3	70	175
2 9	32	176	1 6	62	186
3 0	30	180	1 9	55	192½
3 3	28½	185¼	2 0	50	200
3 6	27	189	2 3	46	207
3 9	26	195	2 6	42½	212½
4 0	25	200	2 9	39½	217¼
4 6	23	207	3 0	37	222
5 0	21½	215	3 3	35	228½
5 6	20	220	3 6	33	231
6 0	19	228	3 9	31	232½
6 6	18¼	237¼	4 0	29½	236
7 0	17½	245	4 6	27	243
8 0	16	256	5 0	24¾	247½

The useful effect of steam engines, independent of locomotives, are estimated in terms of horses' power, one horse's power being an equivalent to 33,000 lbs. Avoirdupois, raised through one foot per minute; but the density of the steam taken into calculation causes a distinction of terms of expressed effect, the one being taken at a constant uniform pressure of 7 lbs. per square inch, which constitute nominal horses' power; the other is the mean effective pressure of steam taken by an Indicator, and called actual horses' power. The following are the general relative rules:—

RULE 1.—Divide the product of 33000 multiplied by the required number of horses' power, by the product of the velocity in feet per minute, multiplied by 7 lbs. per square inch, and the quotient is the piston's area in square inches.

RULE 2.—Multiply the piston's area in square inches by its velocity in feet per minute and by 7 lbs.; divide the product by 33000, and the quotient is the expressed effect in nominal horses' power.

Ex. 1. Required the diameter of cylinder for a condensing engine of 24 nominal horses' power, the length of stroke being 4½ feet, or 207 feet velocity per minute.

$$\frac{33000 \times 24}{207 \times 7} = \frac{792000}{1449} = 546{\cdot}6 \text{ inches area, or } 26\tfrac{3}{8} \text{ inches diameter.}$$

Ex. 2. What is the power of a condensing engine nominally, whose cylinder is 26⅜ inches diameter, and velocity of piston 207 feet per minute?

$$26{\cdot}375^2 \times {\cdot}7854 = 546{\cdot}6 \text{ square inches area.}$$

$$\text{Then } \frac{546{\cdot}6 \times 7 \times 207}{33000} = \frac{792023{\cdot}4}{33000} = 24 \text{ horses' power.}$$

High-pressure, or non-condensing, engines can only properly be estimated in actual horses' power, because it is from the steam's density and velocity that the total amount of useful effect is produced; hence, restricted velocity for calculation of effect is required, which the preceding table of velocities will supply (see page 65), the length of stroke being about three times the cylinder's diameter.

Ex. 1. What must be the diameter of cylinder for a high-pressure engine of 16 horses' power, with a stroke of 3 feet, or 222 feet velocity per minute; the dense steam equal 40 lbs. per square inch, and cut off at ⅓ stroke?

Mean elastic force of steam (as per table, page 70), $= 33{\cdot}86$ lbs. per square inch.

$$\text{Then, } \frac{33000 \times 16}{33{\cdot}86 \times 222} = \frac{528000}{7516{\cdot}92} = 70{\cdot}25 \text{ square inches area, or } 9\tfrac{5}{8} \text{ inches diameter.}$$

Ex. 2. The diameter of the cylinder of a non-condensing engine is 14 inches, length of stroke 3½ feet, dense steam 40 lbs. per square inch, and cut off at ⅝ths of the stroke,—required the actual horses' power.

Area = 154 square inches;
Mean elastic force of steam = 36·15 lbs.;
Velocity of piston in feet per minute = 231.

Then, $\frac{154 \times 36 \cdot 15 \times 231}{33000} = \frac{1286000}{33000} = 38 \cdot 9$ horses' power.

NOTE.—The diameters of circles, consequently the diameters of cylinders, are obtained either by dividing the area by ·7854 and extracting the square root of the quotient, or by multiplying the square root of the area by 1·12837; otherwise refer immediately to the tables of areas and circumferences in this work; but if the tables are not sufficiently extended, divide the area by 4, and twice the diameter opposite the quotient in areas equal the diameter required. Thus, suppose the area $\frac{546 \cdot 6}{4} = 136 \cdot 66$, the diameter of which equal $13\frac{3}{16}$, and twice $13\frac{3}{16} = 26\frac{3}{8}$, the diameter as required.

Approximate Rules relating to non-condensing Steam Engines.

1. To find the power of an engine, the diameter of cylinder and pressure or force of dense steam being given.

RULE.—Multiply the square of the cylinder's diameter in inches by the force of the steam in lbs. per square inch, and by ·003, the product is the number of horses' power nominally that the engine is estimated equal to.

Ex. Required the power of an engine with a cylinder of 9 inches diameter, and steam at 35 lbs. per square inch.

$9^2 = 81 \times 35 = 2835 \times \cdot 003 = 8 \cdot 5$ horses' power.

2. To determine the diameter of cylinder for an engine of a required power nominally, and with a given pressure of steam:—

RULE.—Multiply the required number of horses' power by 334, and divide the product by the force of the steam in lbs. per square inch; the square root of the quotient is the cylinder's diameter in inches.

Ex. What must be the diameter of the cylinder for a 6-horse engine, with steam at 30 lbs. per square inch?

$334 \times 6 = \frac{2004}{30} = \sqrt{66 \cdot 8} = 8 \cdot 173$, or $8\frac{3}{16}$ ins. in diameter.

Table of the diameters of cylinders for condensing engines of nominal horses' power, the strokes of proportionate lengths, and the dense steam 7 lbs. per square inch above atmospheric pressure.

Stationary Engines.					Marine Engines.		
Nominal horses' power.	Diameters of cylinders in inches.	Lengths of strokes in feet.	Number of strokes per minute.	Velocity in feet per minute.	Nominal horses' power.	Diameters of cylinders in inches.	Lengths of strokes in feet.
10	18	3¼	28½	185¼	16	24½	2½
12	19½	3½	27	189	20	26½	"
14	21	"	"	"	25	28½	3
15	21½	3¾	26	195	30	31½	"
16	22	4	25	200	40	36½	3¼
18	23	4¼	24	204	50	39½	3½
20	24½	4½	23	207	60	43	4
24	26¼	4¾	22	209	70	46	4¼
25	26¾	5	21½	215	80	48	4½
28	27½	5½	20	220	90	50	4¾
30	28½	"	"	"	100	52½	5
35	30½	5¾	19½	224¼	110	55	"
40	32½	6	19	228	120	57	5½
45	34¼	"	"	"	130	59	"
50	36	6¼	18½	231¼	150	62½	6
60	39	6½	18	234	200	71½	6½

NOTE.—The diameter of air pump for any stationary engine equal ·67; and the diameter for the same in a marine engine equal ·58 of the cylinder's diameter in inches, at half the stroke of the engine.

Table of the diameters of cylinders for non-condensing engines of actual horses' power, the strokes of proportionate lengths, the dense steam 30 lbs. per square inch, and cut off at $\frac{3}{4}$ths of the stroke.

Horses' power.	Diameters of cylinders in inches.	Lengths of strokes in inches.	Number per minute.	Velocity in feet per minute.
1	$3\frac{1}{8}$	9	100	150
2	$4\frac{1}{4}$	12	80	160
3	5	15	70	175
4	$5\frac{3}{4}$	—	—	—
5	$6\frac{1}{4}$	18	62	186
6	$6\frac{3}{4}$	21	55	$192\frac{1}{2}$
7	$7\frac{1}{8}$	—	—	—
8	$7\frac{5}{8}$	24	50	200
9	$8\frac{1}{8}$	—	—	—
10	$8\frac{3}{8}$	27	46	207
12	$9\frac{1}{8}$	—	—	—
14	$9\frac{3}{4}$	30	$42\frac{1}{2}$	$212\frac{1}{2}$
16	$10\frac{3}{8}$	—	—	—
18	11	33	$39\frac{1}{2}$	$217\frac{1}{4}$
20	$11\frac{1}{2}$	—	—	—
25	$12\frac{3}{4}$	36	37	222

For the necessary production of steam 25 cubic inches of water is required per minute for each horse power, not including waste and other contingencies; hence not less than 35 cubic inches, or about one-eighth of a gallon, can be estimated as a reliable quantity per horse power.

NOTE.—The dense steam at 30 lbs. per square inch, and continued to $\frac{3}{4}$ths of the stroke in a non-condensing engine, is considered a fair average effective power per horse, in a commercial point of view.

Table of the mean elastic force of steam in pounds per square inch in a steam engine, at various grades of expansion.

Initial density of the steam in lbs. per square inch.	Dense steam cut off after the piston has passed through the following parts of the stroke, viz. :—						
Atmospheric pressure not included	$\frac{1}{5}$ or ·2	$\frac{1}{4}$ or ·25	$\frac{2}{5}$ or ·4	$\frac{1}{2}$ or ·5	$\frac{3}{5}$ or ·6	$\frac{3}{4}$ or ·75	$\frac{4}{5}$ or ·8
9	4·69	5·37	6·89	7·62	8·13	8·67	8·80
10	5·22	5·97	7·67	8·46	9·03	9·64	9·78
11	5·74	6·56	8·43	9·31	9·94	10·60	10·76
12	6·26	7·16	9·19	10·16	10·84	11·57	11·74
13	6·78	7·75	9·96	11·01	11·75	12·53	12·72
14	7·31	8·53	10·73	11·85	12·65	13·49	13·97
15	7·83	8·95	11·49	12·69	13.55	14·46	14·68
16	8·35	9·54	12·26	13·54	14·46	15·42	15·66
17	8·87	10·14	13·03	14·39	15·36	16·38	16·63
18	9·39	10·74	13·79	15·24	16·27	17·35	17·61
19	9·92	11·33	14·56	16·81	17·17	18·31	18·59
20	10·44	11·93	15·33	16·93	18·07	19·28	19·57
25	13·04	14·91	19·16	21·16	22·59	24·09	24·46
30	15·65	17·89	22·99	25·39	27·11	28·91	29·35
35	18·26	20·88	26·83	29·63	31·63	33·73	34·24
40	20·87	23·86	30·66	33·86	36·15	38·55	39·04
45	23·48	26·84	34·88	38·09	40·66	43·37	44·03
50	26·09	29·82	38·32	42·33	45·18	48·19	48·92

Ex. If dense steam be admitted to the cylinder of an engine at 35 lbs. per square inch, and cut off when the piston has moved through $\frac{3}{5}$ths of the stroke, the mean elastic pressure during the whole stroke is 31·63 lbs. per square inch, as obtained by initial density and expansive force.

On Steam Boilers.

In the formation or construction of boilers for steam engines, safety and economy are the principal restrictions: capacity for water and steam, superficial heating surface, and sufficient area of fire grate unconfined for ignition of the gases, are laid down as acknowledged rules, viz., 25 to 27 cubic feet capacity, 9 to 12 square feet heating surface, and not less than $\frac{3}{4}$ths of a square foot of fire grate surface to each nominal horse power; but, relative to fire grate surface, it is only where coal is used as fuel that the given dimensions apply. Where wood is the fuel employed, a much greater fire surface is required, particularly in length, so as to receive the billets cut at convenient lengths; and in tropical climates generally, it is highly recommended to form, if possible, a stream of running water in the direction of the flame, fore and aft the boiler, covered in its length everywhere, but immediately under the fire grate. I found the plan very beneficial in India, South America, and in some parts of Australia, where megass or crushed sugar cane, and wood are the only fuels that can at any reasonable rate be obtained. The stream suits the two-fold purpose of carrying away the falling ashes from the fire, and also assists in maintaining a colder current of atmóspheric air to the fire for the support of combustion.

Thin films of water as water spaces in boilers are very objectionable, and ought to be carefully avoided, where possible, in the construction, particularly over fierce fire or flame in a horizontal position; and even vertical water spaces ought to be wider at top than bottom, so as to allow more free egress for the steam in its formation. Again, in flat surfaces stays are unavoidable; but in the wear of boilers anxious examination, whenever an opportunity occurs, ought not to be neglected, as frequently an action takes place around the ends or nuts of some of the stays inside the boiler, as if the plate had been put upon a face plate in a lathe and hollowed out with a round pointed tool.

Table of Dimensions for boilers of a cylindrical form, the engines of nominal horses' power.

Number of horses' power.	Length of boilers in feet.	Length of fire bars in feet & ins.	Diam. of boilers in feet.	Width of furnace. ft. in.		Number of and diam. of flues. ft. in.
1	6	1 7	2¼	1 4	no flue.	—
2	7½	2 0	2½	1 6		—
3	9	2 4	2¾	1 8		—
4	10	2 9	3	1 9		—
5	11	2 11	3½	2 0		—
6	12	3 2	3¾	2 3	one flue.	1 6
8	14	3 8	4	2 4		1 8
10	15½	4 0	4½	2 8		1 11
12	16	4 2	5	2 11		2 0
14	17½	4 7	5¼	3 0		2 3
15	18	4 9	5⅜	3 2		2 4
16	18½	4 10	5½	3 3	two flues	1 7
18	19	5 0	5¾	3 4		1 8
20	20½	5 4	6	3 6		1 9
25	22¼	5 9	6¾	3 11		2 0

NOTE.—For greater powers of engines two boilers are preferable to one of extended dimensions.

To find the indicated pressure, force, or density of steam by a properly adjusted safety valve.

RULE—Multiply the square of the opening in the boiler or narrowest diameter of the valve seat by ·7854, and the product is the area in terms of the dimensions given.

Ex. 1. Let the diameter of opening or seat of valve equal 6⅜ inches, required the area.

$$6{\cdot}375^2 = 40{\cdot}64 \times {\cdot}7854 = 31{\cdot}9 \text{ \&c. square inches.}$$

Suppose an indicated pressure of 12 lbs. per square inch is required, and the weight attached to the valve, the weight of valve and attachments 16½ lbs., what weight will be required?

$$31{\cdot}9 \times 12 = 382{\cdot}8 - 16{\cdot}5 = 366{\cdot}3 \text{ lbs.}$$

If the pressure on a safety valve is to be effected by a lever and weight, or by a lever and spring balance, fix the lever properly into its situation; then, with a spring balance attached immediately at that point of the lever where it rests upon the valve, raise the spring balance by hand until the lever is level, then the index of the spring balance will show the amount of action or downward tendency the lever has, by gravity and leverage, to press down the valve. Multiply the total pressure of steam required upon the valve by the distance between the centre of pin on which the lever moves, and centre of valve; subtract from the product the action of the lever, plus the weight of the valve, divide the remainder by the distance between centre of pin and weight or spring balance attached to the lever, the quotient is the weight required or indicated pressure by spring balance, when steam is just at point of blowing off.

Take the preceding example as the area of valve and pressure of steam required, distance from centre of pin to centre of valve 6½ inches, distance from centre of pin to weight or spring balance 32½ inches, action of lever 14 lbs, weight of valve 7¼ lbs, and required pressure 12 lbs. per square inch.

Area of valve = 31·9 square inches × 12 lbs. = 382·8 lbs. total pressure required.

Action of lever and weight of valve = 14 + 7·25 = 21·25 lbs.; then,

$$382{\cdot}8 \times 6{\cdot}5 = 2488{\cdot}2 - 21{\cdot}25 = \frac{2466{\cdot}95}{32{\cdot}5} = 76 \text{ lbs. to be}$$

suspended by the lever at that point, or indicated weight by spring balance.

Again: suppose all circumstances as above, what will be the pressure on each square inch of the safety valve?

$32{\cdot}5 \times 76 = 2470 + 21{\cdot}25 = 2491{\cdot}25$; and

$31{\cdot}9 \times 6{\cdot}5 = 207{\cdot}35$; hence

$\frac{2491{\cdot}25}{207{\cdot}35} = 12$ lbs. per square inch.

Ex. 2. Suppose the diameter of a safety valve equal 4⅜ inches, the distance between centre of pin and centre of valve 5 inches, distance between centre of pin and point on the lever at which the weight is suspended equal 30 inches, weight of valve and action of lever 9 lbs., weight or indicated pressure by spring balance 76 lbs., required the pressure in lbs. per square inch on the valve.

$$4{\cdot}375^2 \times {\cdot}7854 = 15 \text{ inches area,}$$

$$\text{and } 76 \times 30 + 9 = 2239, \text{ also } 15 \times 5 = 75;$$

$$\text{hence } \frac{2289}{75} = 30{\cdot}52 \text{ lbs. per square inch.}$$

Again, suppose the pressure is to be reduced to 25 lbs. per square inch, under the same circumstances; to what distance on the lever from the centre of pin must the weight or spring balance be placed?

$$15 \times 25 - 9 = 366 \times 5 = \frac{1830}{76} = 24 \text{ inches.}$$

Sometimes where it is inconvenient, for the want of a spring balance, to ascertain the action of the lever on a safety valve, the lever is extended in length beyond its pin or fulcrum on which it moves, and a small ball of any metal attached, as a counterpoise to the lever.

As a rule for the proportioning of safety valves with levers, the distance between fulcrum and centre of valve equal the diameter of the valve, and the distance between weight or spring balance as many times the valve's diameter as there are square inches in its area.

ON LOCOMOTIVE ENGINES.

Table of co-efficients for facilitating the computation of effect by Locomotive Engines.

Lengths of strokes in inches	Diameters of Driving Wheels in Feet.						
	4	4½	5	5½	6	6½	7
	Co-efficients.						
20	·2652	·2393	·2122	·1929	·1768	·1632	·1516
19	·2519	·2273	·2016	·1832	·1679	·1550	·1440
18	·2386	·2153	·1910	·1736	·1591	·1468	·1364
17	·2254	·2034	·1803	·1640	·1503	·1387	·1288
16	·2121	·1914	·1697	·1543	·1415	·1305	·1213
15	·1989	·1795	·1591	·1447	·1326	·1224	·1137
14	·1856	·1675	·1485	·1350	·1237	·1141	·1061
13	·1724	·1555	·1379	·1254	·1149	·1061	·0985
12	·1591	·1436	·1273	·1157	·1061	·0979	·0909

1. To determine the amount of tractive power a locomotive engine is capable of exerting on a level line of railway with a given force or pressure of steam, the following being given, viz.:—

Diameters of cylinders.
Lengths of strokes.
Diameters of driving wheels.
Indicated force or density of steam.
Pounds per ton of tractive power.

Rule.—Multiply the sum of the areas of the pistons in inches by the given pressure of steam in lbs., and by the co-efficient in the table coinciding with the length of stroke and diameters of driving wheels; the product is the total amount of tractive power in lbs.—Divide the product by the tractive power per ton in lbs., and the quotient is the gross load the engine is equal to in tons on a level railway.

Ex. Suppose an engine with cylinders of 13 inches diameter, strokes 18 inches in length, driving wheels $5\frac{1}{2}$ feet in diameter, and steam at 40 lbs. per square inch, required the gross load in tons the engine's power is equal to.

$18^2 \times \cdot7854 = 132\cdot7$ inches in area.
× 2 in number.
265·4
× 40 lbs. per square inch.
10616|0
× ·1736 co-efficient.
1842·9376 or 1843 lbs. tractive power.

Then 1843 ÷ 9·5 = 194 tons gross load; and suppose the engine and tender equal 18 tons,—194 − 18 = 176 tons weight of train.

2. To ascertain what pressure of steam is necessary for a locomotive engine of given weight and dimensions, with a known weight of train attached.

Rule.—Multiply the sum of the areas of the cylinders by the proper co-efficient, as before described, for a divisor; again multiply the gross load of the train in tons by the tractive power in lbs. per ton; divide the product by the divisor, and the quotient is the indicated pressure of steam required in lbs. per square inch.

Ex. An engine and tender of 18 tons in weight, and train 176, or gross weight 194 tons, what force of steam per square inch will be required with the above engine to transport that load upon a level line?

265·4 sum of the two areas.
× ·1736 co-efficient.
15924
7962
18578
2654
46·|07344

194 tons gross load.
× 9·5 lbs. tractive power per ton.
970
1746
1843·0

Hence 1843 ÷ 46 = 40 lbs. per square inch.

In ascending any inclined plane with an engine, the weight or resistance to traction is augmented by gravity as the rise or incline of the plane is to the height; hence if 1 ton, or 2240 lbs., be the unit of weight, $9\frac{1}{2}$ lbs. the unit of traction per ton upon a level line, and 1 in 350 the inclination of the plane, then $2240 \div 350 = 6{\cdot}4$, and $9{\cdot}5 + 6{\cdot}4 = 15{\cdot}9$ lbs. or the force of traction for the same weight upon the incline.

Again, if the train be descending, the force of traction is diminished in an equal ratio, and the train accelerated by gravity; thus, $9{\cdot}5 - 6{\cdot}4 = 3{\cdot}1$ lbs. required for traction on the descending plane.

The resistance to any flat surface 1 foot square passing through a still atmosphere at about 1 mile per hour equal ·005 lbs. Avoir.—and the resistance increases as the square of the velocity. Hence, if a train expose an opposing frontage of 20 square feet at a velocity of 5 miles per hour, $5^2 \times 20 \times {\cdot}005 = 2$ lbs. per hour; but if the velocity be increased to 25 miles per hour, the opposing force of resistance on the same frontage equals $25^2 \times 20 \times {\cdot}005 = 62{\cdot}5$ lbs.

To find the time and distance one railway train will overtake another, their rate of speed being known:—

Rule.—As the difference of the speed of the two bodies in motion is to the distance gone by one, so is the motion of the quicker body to the distance, or term required.

Ex. Suppose a train to be started at a given time, and to continue at the rate of 27 miles per hour; in 35 minutes after, a dispatch train is sent to overtake the first, at a continued speed of 33 miles per hour; how far will the first have gone when the second overtakes it?

$33 - 27 = 6$, and $27 \div 60 = {\cdot}42$ miles per minute, the speed of first train;

Then $\cdot 42 \times 35 = 14{\cdot}7$, and $6 : 14{\cdot}7 :: 35 : 85{\cdot}75$ miles distant when overtaken;

And $6 : {\cdot}42 :: 35 : 2{\cdot}45$ hours, or 2 hours 27 minutes from the time of second train.

Useful notes connected with steam engines generally.

The proper length for the connecting rod of a beam engine, is the perpendicular distance between centre of beam axis and centre of fly wheel shaft.

The proper length for the side rods of a lever engine, is the perpendicular distance between the centre of lever and centre of piston cross-head at half stroke.

The proper length for connecting rods of direct action engines is, the distance between the centre of crank axle and centre of piston cross-head at half stroke.

The proper length for an eccentric rod is, the distance between centre of fly wheel shaft, or centre of revolution, and centre of stud in traverse shaft, when the valve is at half stroke.

To determine the proper velocity for the governor or regulator of a steam engine, or other motive power, the length of pendulums being given :—

Rule.—Divide 375 by twice the square root of the pendulum's length, and the quotient is the number of revolutions per minute.

Ex. What number of revolutions ought a governor to make per minute, whose pendulums are 24 inches in length?

$\sqrt{24} = 4{\cdot}899 \times 2 = 9{\cdot}798$, and $375 \div 9{\cdot}798 = 38{\cdot}27$ revolutions per minute.

To find the proper length of pendulums for a governor, when the number of revolutions per minute are given :—

Rule.—Divide 375 by twice the number of revolutions per minute, and the square of the quotient is the length of pendulums required.

Ex. When the given velocity for a governor is 38·27 revolutions per minute, what must be the length of pendulums?

$38{\cdot}27 \times 2 = 76{\cdot}54$, and $375 \div 76{\cdot}54 = 4{\cdot}9^2 = 24$ inches in length.

The governor of an engine is required to make 52 revolutions per minute during the same time the engine makes

66; on the fly-wheel shaft is fixed a 12 inch pulley, and on the bottom end of governor spindle a bevel wheel containing 36 teeth; required the diameter of intermediate pulley, and also the number of teeth in intermediate wheel by which to effect the proper velocity.

66 × 52 = √ 3432 = 58·58 ratio of velocities;

Then 66 × 12 = 792 ÷ 58·58 = 13·53 inches, diameter of intermediate pulley;

And 52 × 36 = 18720 ÷ 58·58 = 32 teeth in the intermediate wheel.

The first driving wheel from an engine or other motive power is 5 feet 6 inches in diameter at the pitch line, and contains 83 teeth; the engine makes 25 revolutions per minute, and the first line of shafting is to make 36 in the same time; what distance apart from centre to centre must the shafts be placed, and what must be the diameter of the other wheel at the pitch circle?

5½ feet = 66 inches ÷ 2 = 33;

Then 33 × 25 = 825 ÷ 36 = 22·9 × 2 = 45·8 inches, diameter of second or driven wheel;

And 33 + 22·9 = 55·9 inches distance of shafts from centre to centre.

Suppose a wheel or pulley of any given diameter or number of teeth, and at any given velocity—say, in this example, 45 revolutions per minute—what must be the diameter of another to be driven by it, and to make 118 revolutions in the same time?

118 ÷ 45 = 2·62 ratio of velocities.

Let the first wheel or pulley equal 36 inches diameter; then 36 ÷ 2·62 = 13·74, or 13¾ inches of smaller wheel or pulley; and if it be a toothed wheel, it must contain 14 teeth, being the nearest number.

Observe that intermediate wheels, of whatever number of teeth, whereby to communicate motion to another, at any distance apart, cause no variation in velocity, otherwise than would take place were the first and last in immediate contact

When a toothed wheel is caused to produce circular motion by the constant revolutions of a single-threaded screw, the number of revolutions of the screw to one of the wheel equal the number of teeth in the wheel, and as the number of threads in the screw is increased; so is the velocity of the wheel.

Promiscuous gleanings of rules, examples, and observations, for practical application of capacity, solidity, and density.

(See Table of Approximations, p. 21, relative to the following examples).

1. A rectangular cistern is in length $8\frac{1}{2}$ feet, in width $5\frac{1}{4}$ feet, and in depth 4 feet; what is its capacity in cubic feet and also in imperial gallons?

$$8{\cdot}5 \times 5{\cdot}25 \times 4 = 178{\cdot}5 \text{ cubic feet, and}$$
$$178{\cdot}5 \times 6{\cdot}232 = 1112{\cdot}412 \text{ gallons.}$$

2. A rectangular cistern $7\frac{1}{4}$ feet in length, $4\frac{1}{2}$ feet in width, the depth is required, so that it may be capable of containing 520 gallons.

$7{\cdot}25 \times 4{\cdot}5 \times 6{\cdot}232 = 203{\cdot}318$, and $\frac{520}{203{\cdot}318} = 2{\cdot}557$ feet in depth.

3. In a circular sinking in the earth of 4 feet 9 inches diameter, and 35 feet in depth, how many cubic yards excavated in its formation?

$$4{\cdot}75^2 \times 35 \times {\cdot}02909 = 22{\cdot}973 \text{ cubic yards.}$$

Suppose water to spring up in the above sinking until it attained a height of $16\frac{1}{2}$ feet, how many gallons are therein contained, and how many gallons at each inch in depth?

$4{\cdot}75^2 \times 16{\cdot}5 \times 4{\cdot}896 = 1822{\cdot}162$ gallons the whole quantity, and $4{\cdot}75$ feet $= 57$ inches diameter.

Then $57^2 \times {\cdot}002832 = 9{\cdot}25$ gallons at each inch in depth.

4. A cylindrical cistern of sufficient capacity is to be formed so as to be capable of containing 12500 gallons, the depth to be 10 feet, required the diameter.

$4{\cdot}895 \times 10 = 48{\cdot}95$ and $\frac{12500}{48{\cdot}95} = \sqrt{255{\cdot}3} = 15{\cdot}96$ feet diameter.

5. What diameter must I make a cylinder to contain 5 imperial gallons, the height or depth being intended 20 inches?

$$\frac{353 \times 5}{20} = \sqrt{88{\cdot}25} = 9{\cdot}4 \text{ inches diameter.}$$

6. What must be the diameter of a leaden ball to weigh 72 lbs. Avoirdupois?

$$\cdot5236 \times \cdot415 = \cdot217 \text{ and } \frac{72}{\cdot217} = 6{\cdot}91 \text{ inches diameter.}$$

NOTE.—The cube of the diameter of any sphere or ball multiplied by ·5236 equal its solidity, and ·415 equal the weight of a cubic inch of lead in lbs. Avoirdupois.

7. The length of a cast iron round solid shaft is $9\frac{1}{2}$ feet and its diameter 6 inches, what is its estimated weight?

When the length is feet and the diameter inches, the multiplier is 2·48.

Then $6^2 \times 2{\cdot}48 \times 9{\cdot}5 = 848{\cdot}16$ lbs. Avoirdupois.

·009 is the approximate for cwts. (see table page 21), $848{\cdot}16 \times \cdot009 = 7{\cdot}633$ cwts.

Let the same be of wrought iron, required the weight?

The multiplier for wrought iron is 2·6.

Then $6^2 \times 2{\cdot}65 \times 9{\cdot}5 = 906{\cdot}3$ lbs. Avoirdupois, and $906{\cdot}3 \times \cdot009 = 8{\cdot}1567$ cwts.

8. The internal diameter of a fly wheel rim of cast iron is 8 feet 4 inches, or 100 inches, the breadth of rim is 5 inches, and thickness 4, what is its weight in cwts.?

$$100 + 5 = 105 \times 5 \times 4 \times \cdot0074 = 15{\cdot}54 \text{ cwts.}$$

9. What ought the weight to be for the rim of a fly wheel proper for a steam engine of 20 horses' power, the wheel 16 feet external diameter, and velocity 21 revolutions per minute?

$$1368 \text{ (constant number)} \times 20 = 27360, \text{ and}$$

$$21 \times 16 = 336, \text{ hence } \frac{27360}{336} = 81{\cdot}4 \text{ cwts.}$$

Properties of the Circle.

10. It is the most capacious geometrical figure known, bounded by equal perimeter or outline.

The diameter of a circle equal in area to 1 square unit is 1·1284, the circumference of which equal 3·545 in terms of the diameter.

A square of equal area is bounded by 4. And a rectangle of equal area, but its length four times its width, equal 5 in boundary line, inclosing only the same amount of areal space.

Circles are in proportion as the squares of their diameters. Any circle twice the diameter of another, contains four times the area of the other; hence, if the area of any circle is required to be divided into a given number of equal parts, or areas of the whole, square the circle's diameter, divide into the number of parts required, and the square root of each is the diameter of each, or as many as may be required in one area can be added into one sum, and the square root of that area equal the diameter.

The areal unit of square measure being 1, the areal unit of a circle equal ·7854, or half the circumference multiplied by half the diameter; hence, the area of any circle is equal to the square of its diameter multiplied by ·7854.

11. The diameter of a circle equal the sum of the squares of the chord of its segment and versed sine, divided by the versed sine; thus, suppose a segment whose chord is 18 and versed sine 6.

$18^2 + 6^2 = 360 \div 6 = 60$ the diameter of the circle, of which it is a part.

When the length of chord and diameter of circle is given, to find the versed sine or height of the segment:—

RULE.—To the radius of circle add half the length of chord, multiply the sum by their difference, and the square root of the product subtracted from the radius equal the versed sine.

Suppose the chord of the segment is in a circle of 60 feet diameter, required the versed sine.

$$\overline{30 + 18} = 48, \text{ and } 30 - 18 = 12, \text{ then}$$

$$48 \times 12 = \sqrt{576} = 24, \text{ and } 30 - 24 = 6, \text{ the versed sine}$$

Table of versed sines, chords, and areas of circular segments, the semi-circle being unity, or $\frac{\cdot 7854}{2} = \cdot 3927$.

Heights of segments in 100ths, of the radius from circumference.	Chords of segments, the diameter of circle being unity, or 1.	Areas of segments, the area of semi-circle being unity, or 1.	Area of each 100th of the semi-circle on the radius from circumference.
·01	·142	·00042	·00042
·02	·198	·00125	·00085
·03	·241	·00234	·00109
·04	·279	·00364	·00130
·05	·312	·00512	·00148
·06	·339	·00677	·00165
·07	·366	·00857	·00180
·08	·391	·01050	·00193
·09	·414	·01254	·00204
·10	·438	·01468	·00214
·11	·456	·01690	·00222
·12	·476	·01922	·00232
·13	·494	·02163	·00241
·14	·512	·02413	·00250
·15	·528	·02672	·00259
·16	·545	·02940	·00268
·17	·560	·03216	·00276
·18	·576	·03500	·00284
·19	·590	·03791	·00291
·20	·600	·04088	·00297
·21	·614	·04390	·00302
·22	·627	·04699	·00309
·23	·639	·05015	·00316
·24	·650	·05338	·00323
·25	·662	·05667	·00329

Heights of segments in 100ths, of the radius from circumference.	Chords of segments, the diameter of circle being unity, or 1.	Areas of segments, the area of semicircle being unity, or 1.	Area of each 100th of the semicircle on the radius from circumference.
·26	·673	·06001	·00343
·27	·684	·06340	·00339
·28	·696	·06684	·00344
·29	·705	·07033	·00349
·30	·716	·07387	·00354
·31	·725	·07746	.00359
·32	·734	·08110	·00364
·33	·743	·084795	·003695
·34	·752	·08854	·003745
·35	·760	·09232	·00378
·36	·769	·09614	·00382
·37	·778	·10000	·00386
·38	·787	·10390	·00390
·39	·794	·10784	·00394
·40	·800	·11182	·00398
·41	·807	·11584	·00402
·42	·815	·11990	·00406
·43	·823	·12400	·00410
·44	·828	·12813	·00413
·45	·836	·13229	·00416
·46	·842	·13648	·00419
·47	·849	·14070	·00422
·48	·855	·14495	·00425
·49	·861	·14923	·00428
·50	·865	·15354	·00431
·51	·872	·15788	·00433
·52	·878	·16225	·00437
·53	·883	.16664	·00439
·54	·888	·171065	·004425
·55	·894	·17552	·004455

Heights of segments in 100ths, of the radius from circumference.	Chords of segments, the diameter of circle being unity, or 1.	Areas of segments, the area of semicircle being unity, or 1.	Area of each 100th of the semicircle on the radius from circumference.
·56	·898	·180005	·004485
·57	.903	·18451	·004505
·58	·908	·189045	·004535
·59	·912	·19360	·004555
·60	·917	·19817	·00457
·61	·922	·202755	·004585
·62	·926	·20736	·004605
·63	·931	·211995	·004635
·64	·934	·21665	·004655
·65	·939	·221325	·004675
·66	·943	·22602	·004695
·67	·946	·230735	·004715
·68	·949	·23547	·00475
·69	·953	·24022	·00476
·70	·955	·24498	·00477
·71	·958	·24975	·00479
·72	·961	·25455	·00481
·73	·964	·25935	·00483
·74	·967	·26418	·00484
·75	·970	·26902	·00485
·76	·973	·27387	·00486
·77	·975	·27873	·00487
·78	·977	·28360	·00488
·79	·979	·28848	·00489
·80	·981	·29337	·004875
·81	·983	·298275	·004905
·82	·985	·303198	·004923
·83	·987	·308130	·004932
·84	·989	·313066	·004936
·85	·991	·318008	·004942

Heights of segments in 100ths, of the radius from circumference.	Chords of segments, the diameter of circle being unity, or 1.	Areas of segments, the area of semicircle being unity, or 1.	Area of each 100th of the semicircle on the radius from circumference.
·86	·993	·322953	·004945
·87	·994	·327902	·004949
·88	·995	·832858	·004956
·89	·996	·337817	·004959
·90	·997	·342780	·004963
·91	·998	·347754	·004974
·92	·9982	·352739	·004985
·93	·9983	·357729	·004990
·94	·9984	·362721	·004992
·95	·9985	·367715	·004994
·96	·9986	·372710	·004995
·97	·9987	·377706	·004996
·98	·9988	·382703	·004997
·99	·9999	·387701	·004998
1·00	1·0000	·392700	·004999

Application of the preceding Table to practical purposes.

To find the area of the segment of a circle, the versed sine and diameter of circle being given.

Rule.—Divide the versed sine by the radius of the circle, the quotient is the versed sine in 100ths of unity; multiply the corresponding tabular area of unity by the square of the circle's diameter, and the product is the area of the segment in terms of the diameter.

Ex. The diameter of a circle equal 50 feet, required the area of a corresponding segment whose versed sine equal 18.

$\frac{18}{25} = \cdot 72$,—In the first column and opposite to which in the third column is ·25455, or area of unity; hence, $\cdot 25455 \times 50^2 = 636\cdot 35$ square feet, the area.

The diameter of a circle and area of a required corresponding segment being given, to find the height or versed sine of the segment requisite to be cut off.

RULE.—Divide the given area of the segment by the square of the circle's diameter, the quotient is the tabular area of unity, opposite to which, under heights of segments, is the versed sine of unity ; multiply this versed sine by the radius of the circle, and the product is the versed sine of the required segment in terms of the diameter.

Ex. Suppose the diameter of a circle equal 6 feet, and from which a segment containing 5 areal feet is required, what must be the height or versed sine of the segment ?

$\frac{5}{36} = \cdot13888$, the nearest tabular area, is ·14070, and opposite to which is ·47. Hence $\cdot47 \times 3 = 1\cdot41$ feet the height, or versed sine required.

To find the chord of a segment, the diameter of circle and versed sine of the segment being given.

RULE.—Divide the versed sine by the radius of the circle, ; multiply the tabular length of chord (corresponding to the quotient) by the diameter of the circle, and the product is the chord of the segment in terms of the diameter.

Ex. Suppose a circle whose diameter is 40 feet and versed sine 10, required the length of chord.

$\frac{10}{20} = \cdot50$, opposite to which in the table (under chords of segments) is ·865 ; hence, $\cdot865 \times 40 = 34\cdot6$ feet, the length of chord.

Combined Examples.

1. Required the area of the segment of a circle whose length of chord equal 20 feet, and versed sine 4.

$\frac{20}{2} = 10^2 + 4^2 = \frac{116}{8} = 14\cdot5$ the radius, then

$\frac{4}{14\cdot5} = \cdot2758$, tabular area for $\cdot27 = \cdot0634$, and opposite to it in next column is $\cdot00339 \times \cdot0058 = \cdot0019662 + \cdot0634 = \cdot0654$; hence, 29 feet, or the diameter squared $= 841$, and $\cdot0654 \times 841 = 55\cdot0014$ square feet the area of segment.

2. An iron cylindrical boiler 20 feet in length and 5½ feet in diameter, weighing 2¾ tons, is to be made securely water tight, so that it may be floated up a river of fresh water to its destination; required the quantity of water that it will displace, and the depth of its greatest immersion on the radius.

1 ton = 2240 lbs. × 2·75 = 6160 total weight in lbs.;
And 1 cubic foot of fresh water = 62 5 lbs.; hence

$\frac{6160}{62·5}$ = 98·56 cubic feet of water displaced,

and $\frac{98·56}{20}$ = 4·928 areal feet of segment immersed;

Then $\frac{4·928}{5·5^2}$ = ·16291 tabular area, the nearest to which is ·16225; opposite to it in the first column, or heights of segments, is ·52, and ·52 × 2·75 or radius = 1·43 feet, its greatest depth of immersion if the weights of each end be equal.

Rules for Circumferences and Areas of Circles.

For the sake of brevity, the following tables are not extended beyond 40 inches, larger diameters not being frequently required in practice; and when any hurried answer is required, and not found in the tables, half its diameter, as in the following example, will generally expedite.

Let the following be required relative to a 50-inch circle, half of 50 = 25.

As per Table.

Circum.	of 25 = 78·5398 × 2	= 157·0796 cir. of 50.
Square	of 25 = 625 × 2	= 2500 square of 50.
Cube	of 25 = 1562 × 8	= 125000 cube of 50.
Area	of 25 = 490·8739 × 4	= 1963·4956 area of 50.
Side of = sq.	of 25 = 22·1557 × 2	= 44·3114 side of = sq. of 50

and so of any other diameter, and doubling the diameter again if required.

TABLES OF CIRCUMFERENCES AND AREAS OF CIRCLES.

Dia. or Root.	Circum.	Square.	Cube.	Area.	Side of = Square.
1/16	·1963	·0039	·00024	·0030	·0554
1/8	·3927	·0156	·00195	·0122	·1107
3/16	·5890	·0351	·00659	·0276	·1661
1/4	·7854	·0625	·01562	·0490	·2115
5/16	·9817	·0976	·03051	·0767	·2669
3/8	1·1781	·1406	·05273	·1104	·3223
7/16	1·3744	·1914	·08374	·1503	·3771
1/2	1·5708	·25	·125	·1963	·4331
9/16	1·7671	·3164	·17797	·2485	·4995
5/8	1·9635	·3906	·24414	·3068	·5438
11/16	2·1598	·4726	·32495	·3712	·6093
3/4	2·3562	·5625	·42187	·4417	·6646
13/16	2·5525	·6601	·53637	·5185	·7200
7/8	2·7489	·7656	·66992	·6013	·7754
15/16	2·9452	·8789	·81397	·6903	·8308
1 *in.*	3·1416	1	1	·7854	·8862
1/16	3·3379	1·1289	1·19946	·8861	·9416
1/8	3·5343	1·2656	1·42381	·9940	·9969
3/16	3·7306	1·4101	1·67456	1·1075	1·0524
1/4	3·9270	1·5625	1·95312	1·2271	1·0775
5/16	4·1233	1·7226	2·26098	1·3529	1·1631
3/8	4·3197	1·8906	2·59960	1·4848	1·2185
7/16	4·5160	2·0664	2·97045	1·6229	1·2740
1½	4·7124	2·25	3·375	1·7671	1·3293
9/16	4·9087	2·4414	3·81469	1·9175	1·3846
5/8	5·1051	2·6406	4·29101	2·0739	1·4401
11/16	5·3014	2·8476	4·80541	2·2365	1·4954
3/4	5·4978	3·0625	5·35937	2·4052	1·5508
13/16	5·6941	3·2851	5·95434	2·5801	1·6062
7/8	5·8905	3·5156	6·59179	2·7611	1·6616
15/16	6·0868	3·7539	7·27319	2·9488	1·7170

Dia. or Root.	Circum.	Square.	Cube.	Area.	Side of = square.
2 *in.*	6·2832	4	8	3·1416	1·7724
$\frac{1}{16}$	6·4795	4·2539	8·7736	3·3411	1·8278
$\frac{1}{8}$	6·6759	4·5156	9·5957	3·5465	1·8831
$\frac{3}{16}$	6·8722	4·7851	10·4675	3·7582	1·9385
$\frac{1}{4}$	7·0686	5·0625	11·3906	3·9760	1·9939
$\frac{5}{16}$	7·2649	5·3476	12·3663	4·2001	2·0493
$\frac{3}{8}$	7·4613	5·6406	13·3964	4·4302	2·1047
$\frac{7}{16}$	7·6576	5·9414	14·4822	4·6664	2·1601
2½	7·8540	6·25	15·625	4·9087	2·2155
$\frac{9}{16}$	8·0503	6·5664	16·8265	5·1573	2·2709
$\frac{5}{8}$	8·2467	6·8906	18·0878	5·4119	2·3262
$\frac{11}{16}$	8·4430	7·2226	19·4108	5·6727	2·3816
$\frac{3}{4}$	8·6394	7·5625	20·7968	5·9395	2·4370
$\frac{13}{16}$	8·8357	7·9101	22·2472	6·2126	2·4924
$\frac{7}{8}$	9·0321	8·2656	23·7636	6·4918	2·5478
$\frac{15}{16}$	9·2284	8·6289	25·3474	6·7772	2·6032
3 *in.*	9·4248	9	27	7·0686	2·6586
$\frac{1}{16}$	9·6211	9·3789	28·7228	7·3662	2·7140
$\frac{1}{8}$	9·8175	9·7656	30·5175	7·6699	2·7694
$\frac{3}{16}$	10·0138	10·1601	32·3853	7·9798	2·8247
$\frac{1}{4}$	10·2102	10·5625	34·3281	8·2957	2·8801
$\frac{5}{16}$	10·4065	10·9726	36·3467	8·6179	2·9355
$\frac{3}{8}$	11·6029	11·3906	38·4433	8·9462	2·9909
$\frac{7}{16}$	11·7992	11·8164	40·6178	9·2806	3·0463
3½	10·9956	12·25	42·875	9·6211	3·1017
$\frac{9}{16}$	11·1919	12·6914	45·2031	9·9678	3·1570
$\frac{5}{8}$	11·3883	13·1406	47·6347	10·3206	3·2124
$\frac{11}{16}$	11·5846	13·5976	49·9461	10·6796	3·2678
$\frac{3}{4}$	11·7810	14·0625	52·7343	11·0446	3·3232
$\frac{13}{16}$	11·9773	14·5351	55·3930	11·4159	3·3786
$\frac{7}{8}$	12·1737	15·1056	58·1855	11·7932	3·4340
$\frac{15}{16}$	12·3700	15·5039	61·0256	12·1768	3·4984

Dia. or Root.	Circum.	Square.	Cube.	Area.	Side of = square.
4 *in.*	12·5664	16	64	12·5664	3·5448
1/16	12·7627	16·5039	67·0471	12·9622	3·6002
1/8	12·9591	17·0156	70·1894	13·3640	3·6555
3/16	13·1554	17·5351	73·4282	13·7721	3·7110
1/4	13·3518	18·0625	76·7656	14·1862	3·7663
5/16	13·5481	18·5976	80·2021	14·6066	3·8217
3/8	13·7445	19·1406	83·7402	15·0331	3·8771
7/16	13·9408	19·6914	87·3804	15·4657	3·9325
4½	14·1372	20·25	91·125	15·9043	3·9880
9/16	14·3335	20·8164	94·9748	16·3492	4·0433
5/8	14·5299	21·3906	98·9316	16·8001	4·0987
11/16	14·7262	21·9726	101·8965	17·2573	4·1541
3/4	14·9226	22·5625	107·1718	17·7205	4·2095
13/16	15·1189	23·1601	111·4679	18·1900	4·2648
7/8	15·3153	23·7656	115·8574	18·6655	4·3202
15/16	15·5716	24·3789	120·2708	19·1472	4·3756
5 *in.*	15·7080	25	125	19·6350	4·4310
1/16	15·9043	25·6289	129·7463	20·1290	4·4864
1/8	16·1007	26·2656	134·6113	20·6290	4·5417
3/16	16·2970	26·9101	138·5961	21·1252	4·5971
1/4	16·4934	27·5625	144·7031	21·6475	4·6525
5/16	16·6897	28·2226	149·9306	22·1661	4·7079
3/8	16·8861	28·8906	155·2871	22·6907	4·7633
7/16	17·0824	29·5664	160·7673	23·2215	4·8187
5½	17·2788	30·25	166·375	23·7583	4·8741
9/16	17·4751	30·9414	172·1115	24·3014	4·9294
5/8	17·6715	31·6406	177·9785	24·8505	4·9848
11/16	17·8678	32·3476	183·9669	25·4058	5·0402
3/4	18·0642	33·0625	190·1093	25·9672	5·0956
13/16	18·2605	33·7851	196·3759	26·5348	5·1510
7/8	18·4569	34·5156	202·7792	27·1085	5·2064
15/16	18·6532	35·2539	209·3130	27·6884	5·2618

Dia. or Root.	Circum.	Square.	Cube.	Area.	Side of = square.
6 *in.*	18·8496	36	216	28·2744	5·3172
$\frac{1}{16}$	19·0459	36·7539	222·8205	28·8665	5·3726
$\frac{1}{8}$	19·2423	37·5156	229·7832	29·4647	5·4280
$\frac{3}{16}$	19·4386	38·2851	236·8890	30·0798	5·4834
$\frac{1}{4}$	19·6350	39·0625	244·1406	30·6796	5·5388
$\frac{5}{16}$	19·8313	39·8476	249·2654	31·2964	5·5942
$\frac{3}{8}$	20·0277	40·6406	259·0839	31·9192	5·6495
$\frac{7}{16}$	20·2240	41·4414	266·7790	32·5481	5·7049
$6\frac{1}{2}$	20·4204	42·25	274·625	33·1831	5·7603
$\frac{9}{16}$	20·6167	43·0664	282·6232	33·8244	5·8157
$\frac{5}{8}$	20·8131	43·8906	290·7753	34·4717	5·8711
$\frac{11}{16}$	21·0094	44·7226	299·0823	35·1252	5·9265
$\frac{3}{4}$	21·2058	45·5625	307·5468	35·7847	5·9819
$\frac{13}{16}$	21·4021	46·4101	316·1688	36·4505	6·0373
$\frac{7}{8}$	21·5985	47·2656	324·9511	37·1224	6·0927
$\frac{15}{16}$	21·7948	48·1289	333·8943	37·8005	6·1480
7 *in.*	21·9912	49	343	38·4846	6·2034
$\frac{1}{16}$	22·1875	49·8789	349·5702	39·1749	6·2588
$\frac{1}{8}$	22·3839	50·7656	361·7040	39·8713	6·3142
$\frac{3}{16}$	22·5802	51·6601	371·3070	40·5469	6·3096
$\frac{1}{4}$	22·7766	52·5625	381·0781	41·2825	6·4350
$\frac{5}{16}$	22·9729	53·4726	391·0184	41·9974	6·4904
$\frac{3}{8}$	23·1693	54·3906	401·1308	42·7184	6·5358
$\frac{7}{16}$	23·3656	55·3164	411·4158	43·4455	6·5912
$7\frac{1}{2}$	23·5620	56·25	421·875	44·1787	6·6465
$\frac{9}{16}$	23·7583	57·1914	432·5100	44·9181	6·7020
$\frac{5}{8}$	23·9547	58·1406	443·3222	45·6636	6·7573
$\frac{11}{16}$	24·1510	59·0976	454·3129	46·4153	6·8127
$\frac{3}{4}$	24·3474	60·0625	465·4843	47·1730	6·8681
$\frac{13}{16}$	24·5437	61·0351	476·8368	47·9370	6·9235
$\frac{7}{8}$	24·7401	62·0156	488·3730	48·7070	6·9789
$\frac{15}{16}$	24·9364	63·0039	500·0935	49·4833	7·0343

Dia. or Root.	Circum.	Square.	Cube.	Area.	Side of = square.
8 *in.*	25·1328	64	512	50·2656	7·0897
1/16	25·3291	65·0039	524·1939	51·0541	7·1451
1/8	25·5255	66·0156	536·3769	51·8486	7·2005
3/16	25·7218	67·0351	548·8499	52·8994	7·2559
1/4	25·9182	68·0625	561·5156	53·4562	7·3112
5/16	26·1145	69·0976	574·3739	54·2748	7·3666
3/8	26·3109	70·1406	587·4277	55·0885	7·4220
7/16	26·5072	71·1914	600·6775	55·9138	7·4774
8½	26·7036	72·25	614·125	56·7451	7·5328
9/16	26·8999	73·3164	627·7717	57·5887	7·5882
5/8	27·0963	74·3906	641·6191	58·4264	7·6436
11/16	27·2926	75·4726	655·6683	59·7762	7·6990
3/4	27·4890	76·5625	669·9218	60·1321	7·7544
13/16	27·6853	77·6601	684·3797	60·9943	7·8098
7/8	27·8817	78·7656	699·0449	61·8625	7·8651
15/16	28·0780	79·8789	713·9177	62·7369	7·9205
9 *in.*	28·2744	81	729	63·6174	7·9760
1/16	28·4707	82·1289	744·2932	64·5041	8·0312
1/8	28·6671	83·2656	759·7988	65·3968	8·0866
3/16	28·8634	84·4101	775·5378	66·2957	8·1420
1/4	29·0598	85·5625	791·4531	67·2007	8·1974
5/16	29·2561	86·7226	807·8043	68·1120	8·2527
3/8	29·4525	87·8906	823·9746	69·0293	8·3081
7/16	29·6488	89·0664	840·5642	69·9528	8·3635
9½	29·8452	90·25	857·375	70·8823	8·4190
9/16	30·0415	91·4414	874·3084	71·8181	8·4743
5/8	30·2379	92·6406	891·6660	72·7599	8·5297
11/16	30·4342	93·8476	909·1487	73·7079	8·5851
3/4	30·6306	95·0625	926·8593	74·6620	8·6405
13/16	30·8269	96·2851	944·7976	75·6223	8·6959
7/8	31·0233	97·5156	962·9667	76·5887	8·7513
15/16	31·2196	98·7539	981·3669	77·5613	8·8066

Dia. or Root.	Circum.	Square.	Cube.	Area.	Side of = square.
10 *in.*	31·4160	100	1000	78·5400	8·8620
⅛	31·8087	102·5156	1037·970	80·5157	8·9728
¼	32·2014	105·0625	1076·890	82·5160	9·0836
⅜	32·5941	107·6406	1116·771	84·5409	9·1943
½	32·9868	110·25	1157·625	86·5903	9·3051
⅝	33·3795	112·8906	1199·462	88·6643	9·4159
¾	33·7722	115·5625	1242·296	90·7627	9·5267
⅞	34·1649	118·2656	1286·138	92·8858	9·6375
11 *in.*	34·5576	121	1331	95·0334	9·7482
⅛	34·9503	123·7656	1376·892	97·2053	9·8590
¼	35·3430	126·5625	1423·828	99·4021	9·9698
⅜	35·7357	129·3906	1471·818	101·6234	10·0806
½	36·1284	132·25	1520·875	103·8691	10·1914
⅝	36·5211	135·1406	1571·009	106·1394	10·3021
¾	36·9138	138·0625	1622·234	108·4342	10·4130
⅞	37·3065	141·0156	1674·560	110·7536	10·5237
12 *in.*	37·6992	144	1728	113·0976	10·6345
⅛	38·0919	147·0156	1782·564	115·4660	10·7453
¼	38·4846	150·0625	1838·265	117·8590	10·8560
⅜	38·8773	153·1406	1895·115	120·2766	10·9668
½	39·2700	156·25	1953·125	122·7187	11·0776
⅝	39·6627	159·3906	2012·306	125·1854	11·1884
¾	40·0554	162·5625	2072·671	127·6765	11·2991
⅞	40·4481	165·7656	2134·232	130·1923	11·4099
13 *in.*	40·8408	169	2197	132·7326	11·5206
⅛	41·2338	172·2656	2260·986	135·2974	11·6314
¼	41·6262	175·5626	2326·203	137·8867	11·7422
⅜	42·0189	178·8906	2392·661	140·5007	11·8530
½	42·4116	182·25	2460·375	143·1391	11·9637
⅝	42·8043	185·6406	2529·353	145·8021	12·0745
¾	43·1970	189·0625	2599·609	148·4896	12·1853
⅞	43·5897	192·5156	2671·154	151·2017	12·2961

Dia. or Root,	Circum.	Square.	Cube.	Area.	Side of = square.
14 *in.*	43·9824	196	2744	153·9384	12·4068
1/8	44·3751	199·5156	2818·157	156·6995	12·5176
1/4	44·7676	203·0625	2893·640	159·4852	12·6284
3/8	45·1605	206·6406	2970·458	162·2956	12·7392
1/2	45·5532	210·25	3048·625	165·1303	12·8500
5/8	45·9459	213·8906	3128·150	167·9896	12·9607
3/4	46·3386	217·5625	3209·046	170·8735	13·0715
7/8	46·7313	221·2656	3291·325	173·7820	13·1823
15 *in.*	47·1240	225	3375	176·7150	13·2930
1/8	47·5167	228·7656	3460·079	179·6725	13·4038
1/4	47·9094	232·5625	3546·578	182·6545	13·5146
3/8	48·3021	236·3906	3633·505	185·6612	13·6254
1/2	48·6948	240·25	3723·875	188·6923	13·7361
5/8	49·0875	244·1406	3814·696	191·7480	13·8470
3/4	49·4802	248·0625	3906·984	194·8282	13·9577
7/8	49·8729	252·0156	4000·747	197·9330	14·0685
16 *in.*	50·2656	256	4096	201·0624	14·1792
1/8	50·6583	260·0156	4192·751	204·2162	14·2900
1/4	51·0510	264·0625	4291·015	207·3946	14·4008
3/8	51·4437	268·1406	4390·802	210·5976	14·5115
1/2	51·8364	272·25	4492·125	213·8251	14·6223
5/8	52·2291	276·3906	4594·993	217·0772	14·7321
3/4	52·6218	280·5625	4699·421	220·3537	14·8439
7/8	53·0145	284·7656	4805·419	223·6549	14·9547
17 *in.*	53·4072	289	4913	226·9806	15·0654
1/8	53·7999	293·2656	5022·173	230·3308	15·1762
1/4	54·1926	297·5625	5132·953	233·7055	15·2869
3/8	54·5853	301·8906	5245·349	237·1049	15·3977
1/2	54·9780	306·25	5359·375	240·5287	15·5085
5/8	55·3707	310·6406	5475·040	243·9771	15·6193
3/4	55·7634	315·0625	5592·359	247·4500	15·7301
7/8	56·1561	319·5156	5711·341	250·9475	15·8408

Dia. or Root.	Circum.	Square.	Cube.	Area.	Side of = Square.
18 *in.*	56·5488	324	5832	254·4696	15·9516
1/8	56·9415	328·5156	5954·345	258·0161	16·0624
1/4	57·3342	333·0625	6078·390	261·5872	16·1732
3/8	57·7269	337·6406	6204·146	265·1829	16·2839
1/2	58·1196	342·25	6331·625	268·8031	16·3947
5/8	58·5123	346·8906	6460·837	272·4479	16·5055
3/4	58·9056	351·5625	6591·796	276·1171	16·6163
7/8	59·2977	356·2656	6724·513	279·8110	16·7270
19 *in.*	59·6904	361	6859	283·5294	16·8378
1/8	60·0831	365·7656	6995·267	287·2723	16·9486
1/4	60·4758	370·5625	7132·328	291·0397	17·0600
3/8	60·8685	375·3906	7273·192	294·8312	17·1701
1/2	61·2612	380·25	7414·875	298·6483	17·2809
5/8	61·6539	385·1406	7558·384	302·4894	17 3917
3/4	62·0466	390·0625	7703·734	306·3550	17·5025
7/8	62·4393	395·0156	7850·935	310·2452	17·6132
20 *in.*	62·8320	400	8000	314·1600	17·7240
1/8	63·2247	405·0156	8150·939	318·0992	17·8348
1/4	63·6174	410·0625	8303·765	322·0630	17·9456
3/8	64·0101	415·1406	8458·489	326 0514	18·0563
1/2	64·4028	420·25	8615·125	330·0643	18·1671
5/8	64·7955	425·3906	8773·681	334·1018	18·2779
3/4	65·1882	430·5625	8934·171	338·1637	18 3887
7/8	65·5809	435·7656	9096·607	342·2503	18·4995
21 *in.*	65·7936	441	9261	346·3614	18·6102
1/8	66·3663	446·2656	9427·360	350·4970	18 7210
1/4	66·7590	451·5625	9595·703	354·6571	18·8318
3/8	67·1517	456·8906	9766·036	358 8419	18·9425
1/2	67·5444	462·25	9938·375	363·0511	19 0533
5/8	67·9371	467·6406	10112·72	367·2849	19·1641
3/4	68·3298	473·0625	10289·11	371·5432	19·2749
7/8	68·7225	478·5156	10467·52	375·8261	19·3857

Dia. or Root	Circum.	Square.	Cube.	Area.	Side of = square.
22 *in.*	69·1152	484	10648	380·1336	19·4964
1/8	69·5079	489·5156	10830·53	384·4655	19·6072
1/4	69·9006	495 0625	11015·14	388·8220	19·7180
3/8	70.2933	500·6406	11201·83	393·2031	19·8287
1/2	70·6860	506·25	11390·62	397·6087	19·9395
5/8	71·0787	511·8906	11581·52	402·0888	20·0503
3/4	71·4714	517·5625	11774·54	406·4935	20·1611
7/8	71·8641	523·2656	11969·70	410·9728	20·2719
23 *in.*	72·2568	529	12167	415·4766	20·3826
1/8	72 6495	534·7656	12366·45	420·0049	20·4934
1/4	73·0422	540 5625	12568·07	424·5577	20·6042
3/8	73·4349	546·3906	12771·88	429·1352	20·7150
1/2	73·8276	552·25	12977·87	433·7371	20·8257
5/8	74·2203	558·1406	13185·98	438·3636	20·9365
3/4	74·6130	564·0625	13396·48	443·0146	21·0473
7/8	75·0057	570·0156	13609·12	447·6992	21·1581
24 *in.*	75·3984	576	13824	452·3904	21·2688
1/8	75·7911	582·0156	14041·126	457·1150	21·3796
1/4	76·1838	588·0625	14260·515	461·8642	21·4904
3/8	76·5765	594·1406	14482·177	466·6380	21·6012
1/2	76·9692	600·25	14706·125	471·4363	21·7119
5/8	77·3619	606·3906	14932·368	476·2592	21 8227
3/4	77·7546	612·5625	15160·921	481·1065	21·9335
7/8	78·1473	618·7656	15391·794	485·9785	22·0443
25 *in.*	78·5400	625	15625	490·8750	22·1550
1/8	78 9327	631·2656	15860·548	495·7960	22·2658
1/4	79·3254	637·5625	16098·453	500·7415	22·3766
3/8	79·7181	643·8906	16338·323	505·7117	22·4873
1/2	80·1108	650·25	16581·375	510·7063	22·5981
5/8	80·5035	656·6406	16826 415	515·7255	22 7089
3/4	80·8962	663·0625	17073·859	520·7692	22·8197
7/8	81·2889	669·5156	17323·716	525·8375	22·9305

Dia. or Root.	Circum.	Square.	Cube.	Area.	Side of = square.
26 *in.*	81·6816	676	17576	530·9304	23·0412
$\frac{1}{8}$	82·0743	682·5156	17830·720	536·0477	23·1520
$\frac{1}{4}$	82·4670	689·0625	18087·890	541·1896	23 0628
$\frac{3}{8}$	82·8597	695·6406	18347·520	546·3561	23·3735
$\frac{1}{2}$	83·2524	702·25	18609·625	551·5471	23·4843
$\frac{5}{8}$	83·6451	708·8906	18874·212	556·7627	23·5951
$\frac{3}{4}$	84·0378	715·5625	19141·296	562·0027	23·7088
$\frac{7}{8}$	84·4305	722·2656	19410·888	567·2674	23·8166
27 *in.*	84·8232	729	19683	572·5566	23·9274
$\frac{1}{8}$	85·2159	735·7656	19957·642	577·8703	24·0382
$\frac{1}{4}$	85·6086	742·5625	20234·828	583·2085	24·1490
$\frac{3}{8}$	86·0013	749·3906	20514·567	588·5714	24·2598
$\frac{1}{2}$	86·3940	756·25	20796·875	593·9587	24·3705
$\frac{5}{8}$	86·7867	763·1406	21081·759	599·3706	24·4813
$\frac{3}{4}$	87·1794	770·0625	21369·234	604·8070	24 5921
$\frac{7}{8}$	87·5721	777·0156	21659·309	610·2680	24·7029
28 *in.*	87·9648	784	21952	615·7536	24·8136
$\frac{1}{8}$	88·3575	791·0156	22247·313	621·2636	24·9244
$\frac{1}{4}$	88·7502	798·0625	22545·265	626·7982	25·0351
$\frac{3}{8}$	89·1429	805·1406	22845·864	632·3574	25·1459
$\frac{1}{2}$	89·5356	812·25	23149·125	637·9411	25·2567
$\frac{5}{8}$	89·9283	819·3906	23455·056	643·5494	25·3675
$\frac{3}{4}$	90·3210	826·5625	23763·671	649·1821	25·4783
$\frac{7}{8}$	90·7137	833·7656	24074·981	654·8395	25·5891
29 *in.*	91·1064	841	24389	660·5214	25·6998
$\frac{1}{8}$	91·4991	848·2656	24705·735	666·2278	25·8106
$\frac{1}{4}$	91·8918	855·5625	25025·203	671·9587	25·9214
$\frac{3}{8}$	92·2845	862·8906	25347·411	677·7143	26·0325
$\frac{1}{2}$	92·6772	870·25	25672·375	683·4943	26·1429
$\frac{5}{8}$	93·0699	877·6406	26000·102	689·2989	26·2537
$\frac{3}{4}$	93·4626	885·0625	26330·609	695·1280	26·3645
$\frac{7}{8}$	93·8553	892·5156	26663·903	700·9817	26·4788

Dia. or Root.	Circum.	Square.	Cube.	Area.	Side of = square.
30 *in.*	94·2480	900	27000	706·8600	26·5860
$\frac{1}{8}$	94·6407	907·5156	27338·907	712·7627	26·6967
$\frac{1}{4}$	95·0334	915·0625	27680·640	718·6900	26·8075
$\frac{3}{8}$	95·4261	922·6406	28025·208	724·6419	26·9183
$\frac{1}{2}$	95·8188	930·25	28372·625	730·6183	27·0291
$\frac{5}{8}$	96·2115	937·8906	28722·899	736·6193	27·1398
$\frac{3}{4}$	96·6042	945·5625	29076·046	742·6447	27·2506
$\frac{7}{8}$	96·9969	953·2656	29432·075	748·6948	27·3614
31 *in.*	97·3896	961	29791	754·7694	27·4722
$\frac{1}{8}$	97·7823	968·7656	30152·829	760·8685	27·5829
$\frac{1}{4}$	98·1750	976·5625	30517·578	766·9921	27·6937
$\frac{3}{8}$	98·5677	984·3906	30885·255	773·1404	27·8045
$\frac{1}{2}$	98·9684	992·25	31255·875	779·3131	27·9153
$\frac{5}{8}$	99·3531	1000·140	31629·446	785·5104	28·0260
$\frac{3}{4}$	99·7458	1008·062	32005·984	791·7322	28·1368
$\frac{7}{8}$	100·1385	1016·015	32385·497	797·9786	28·2476
32 *in.*	100·5312	1024	32768	804·2496	28·3584
$\frac{1}{8}$	100·9240	1032·015	33153·501	810·5450	28·4691
$\frac{1}{4}$	101·3166	1040·062	33542·015	816·8650	28·5799
$\frac{3}{8}$	101·7093	1048·840	33956·314	823·2096	28·6912
$\frac{1}{2}$	102·1020	1056·25	34328·125	829·5787	28·8015
$\frac{5}{8}$	102·4947	1064·390	34725·743	835·9724	28·9122
$\frac{3}{4}$	102·8874	1072·562	35026·421	842·3905	29·0230
$\frac{7}{8}$	103·2801	1080·765	35530·169	848·8333	29·1338
33 *in.*	103·6728	1089	35937	855·3006	29·2446
$\frac{1}{8}$	104·0655	1097·265	36354·928	861·7924	29·3553
$\frac{1}{4}$	104·4582	1105·562	36759·944	868·3087	29·4661
$\frac{3}{8}$	104·8509	1113·890	37256·088	874·8497	29·5769
$\frac{1}{2}$	105·2436	1122·25	37595·375	881·4151	29·6877
$\frac{5}{8}$	105·6363	1130·640	38017·784	888·0051	29·7985
$\frac{3}{4}$	106·0290	1139·062	38443·352	894·6196	29·9092
$\frac{7}{8}$	106·4217	1147·515	38872·088	901·2587	30·0200

Dia. or Root.	Circum.	Square.	Cube.	Area.	Side of = square.
34 *in.*	106·8144	1156	39304	907·9224	30·1308
⅛	107·2071	1164·515	39738·288	914·6105	30·2416
¼	107·5998	1173·062	40177·384	921·3232	30·3523
⅜	107·9925	1181·640	40618·888	928·0605	30·4631
½	108·3852	1190·25	41063·625	934·8223	30·5739
⅝	108·7779	1198·890	41511·576	941·6087	30·6847
¾	109·1706	1207·562	41962·792	948·4195	30·7954
⅞	109·5633	1216·265	42417·256	955·2550	30·9062
35 *in.*	109·9560	1225	42875	962·1150	31·0170
⅛	110·3487	1233·765	43352·016	968·9995	31·1278
¼	110·7414	1242·562	43800·320	975·9085	31·2386
⅜	111·1341	1251·390	44267·944	982·8422	31·3493
½	111·5268	1260·25	44738·875	989·8003	31·4601
⅝	111·9195	1269·140	45213·120	996·7830	31·5709
¾	112·3122	1278·062	45690·728	1003·7902	31·6817
⅞	112·7049	1287·015	46171·680	1010·8220	31·7924
36 *in.*	113·0976	1296	46656	1017·8784	31·9032
⅛	113·4903	1308·015	47252·063	1024·9592	32·0139
¼	113 8830	1314·062	47634·765	1032·0646	32·1247
⅜	114·2757	1323·140	48129·239	1039·1946	32·2355
½	114·6684	1332·25	48627·125	1046·3941	32·3463
⅝	115·0611	1341·390	49128·430	1053·5281	32·4570
¾	115·4538	1350·562	49633·171	1060·7317	32·5678
⅞	115·8465	1359·765	50141·356	1067·9599	32·6786
37 *in.*	116·2392	1369	50653	1075·2126	32·7894
⅛	116·6319	1378·265	51168·110	1082·4898	32·9001
¼	117·0246	1387·562	51686·703	1089·7915	33·0109
⅜	117·4173	1396·890	52208·786	1097·1179	33·0217
½	117·8100	1406·25	52734·375	1104·4687	33·2325
⅝	118·2027	1415·640	53263·477	1111·8441	33·3432
¾	118·5954	1425·062	53796·109	1119·2440	33·4540
⅞	118·9881	1434·515	54332·278	1126·6685	33·5648

Dia. or Root.	Circum.	Square.	Cube.	Area.	Side of = square.
38 *in.*	119·3808	1444	54872	1134·1176	33·6756
⅛	119·7735	1453·515	55415·282	1141·5911	33·7863
¼	120·1662	1463·062	55962·140	1149·0892	33·8971
⅜	120·5589	1472·640	56512·583	1156·6119	34·0079
½	120·9516	1482·25	57066·625	1164·1591	34·1187
⅝	121·3443	1491·890	57624·274	1171·7309	34·2294
¾	121·7370	1501·562	58185·546	1179·3271	34·3402
⅞	122·1297	1511·265	58750·450	1186·9480	34·4510
39 *in.*	122·5224	1521	59319	1194·5934	34·5618
⅛	122·9151	1530·765	59891·204	1202·2633	34·6725
¼	123·3078	1540·562	60466·078	1209·9577	34·7833
⅜	123·7005	1550·390	61046·629	1217·6768	34·8941
½	124·0932	1560·25	61629·875	1225·4203	35·0049
⅝	124·4859	1570·140	62216·822	1233·1884	35·1156
¾	124·8786	1580·062	62807·484	1240·9810	35·2264
⅞	125·2713	1590·015	63401·872	1248·7982	35·3372
40 *in.*	125·6640	1600	64000	1256·6400	35·4480

The Lineal, Square, and Cubic Foot of different Countries, given in British inches.

Countries.	Lineal Foot.	Square Foot.	Cubic Foot.
Austria	12·45	155·002	1929·774
Belgium	11·24	126·337	1420·627
China	12·58	168·256	2116·665
Germany	11·28	127·441	1438·684
Holland	11·16	124·255	1385·070
Italy	12·72	161·798	2058·071
Portugal	12·94	167·547	2168·728
Prussia...	12·19	148·603	1813·162
Rome	11·72	137·358	1609·840
Russia	13·75	189·062	2599·609
Spain......................	11·12	123·654	1378·002
Sweden..................	11·68	136·515	1595·041

NOTE.—The British lineal foot is used generally throughout America, the British West Indies, and Australia.

Table of Commission or Discount.

Rate per cent.	Rate per £ in pence, decimally.	Rate per £ to the nearest fraction of current money.	Rate per shilling in pence, decimally.	Rate per shilling to the nearest fraction of current money.	Rate per cent.	Rate per £ in pence, decimally.	Rate per £ to the nearest fraction of current money.	Rate per shilling in pence, decimally.	Rate per shilling to the nearest fraction of current money.
		s. d.		d.			s. d.		d.
½	1·2	1¼	·06		13	31·2	2 7½	1·56	
⅝	1·5	1½	·075		13½	32·4	2 8½	1·62	
¾	1·8	1¾	·09		14	33·6	2 9½	1·68	
⅞	2·1	2	·105		14½	34·8	2 11	1·74	
1	2·4	2½	·12		15	36·0	3 0	1·8	1¾
1½	3·6	3½	·18		15½	37·2	3 1¼	1·86	
2	4·8	5	·24		16	38·4	3 2½	1·92	
2½	6·0	6	·3	¼	16½	39·6	3 3½	1·98	
3	7·2	7¼	·36		17	40·8	3 5	2·04	2
3½	8·4	8½	·42		17½	42·0	3 6	2·1	
4	9·6	9½	·48		18	43·2	3 7¼	2·16	
4½	10·8	11	·54	½	18½	44·4	3 8½	2·22	
5	12·0	1 0	·6		19	45·6	3 9½	2·28	2¼
5½	13·2	1 1¼	·66		19½	46·8	3 11	2·34	
6	14·4	1 2½	·72		20	48·0	4 0	2·4	
6½	15·6	1 3½	·78	¾	20½	49·2	4 1½	2·46	
7	16·8	1 5	·84		21	50·4	4 2½	2·52	2½
7½	18·0	1 6	·9		21½	51·6	4 3½	2·58	
8	19·2	1 7¼	·96		22	52·8	4 5	2·64	
8½	20·4	1 8½	1·02	1	22½	54·0	4 6	2·7	
9	21·6	1 9½	1·08		23	55·2	4 7¼	2·76	2¾
9½	22·8	1 11	1·14		23½	56·4	4 8½	2·82	
10	24·0	2 0	1·2		24	57·6	4 9½	2·88	
10½	25·2	2 1¼	1·26	1¼	24½	58·8	4 11	2·94	
11	26·4	2 2½	1·32		25	60·0	5 0	3·0	3
11½	27·6	2 3½	1·38		27½	66·0	5 6	3·3	3¼
12	28·8	2 5	1·44		30	72·0	6 0	3·6	3½
12½	30·0	2 6	1·5	1½	35	74·4	6 2½	3·72	3¾

Weights and Numbers of Equivalent Values.

Price per lb.	Per stone of 14lbs.	Per quarter, or 28lbs.	Per cwt., or 112lbs.	Per ton, or 2240lbs.	Per 1000.	Per gross, or 144.	Per hund. or 120.	Per hund. or 100.	Per score, or 20.	Per dozen, or 12.	Price for 1.
d.	s. d.	£ s. d.	£ s. d.	£ s. d.	£ s. d.	£ s.	£ s. d.	£ s d.	s. d.	s. d.	d.
0¼	0 3½	0 0 7	0 2 4	2 6 8	1 0 10	0 3	0 2 6	0 2 1	0 5	0 3	0¼
0½	0 7	0 1 2	0 4 8	4 13 4	2 1 8	0 6	0 5 0	0 4 2	0 10	0 6	0½
0¾	0 10½	0 1 9	0 7 0	7 0 0	3 2 6	0 9	0 7 6	0 6 3	1 3	0 9	0¾
1	1 2	0 2 4	0 9 4	9 6 8	4 3 4	0 12	0 10 0	0 8 4	1 8	1 0	1
1¼	1 5½	0 2 11	0 11 8	11 13 4	5 4 2	0 15	0 12 6	0 10 5	2 1	1 3	1¼
1½	1 9	0 3 6	0 14 0	14 0 0	6 5 0	0 18	0 15 0	0 12 6	2 6	1 6	1½
1¾	2 0½	0 4 1	0 16 4	17 6 8	7 5 10	1 1	0 17 6	0 14 7	2 11	1 9	1¾
2	2 4	0 4 8	0 18 8	18 13 4	8 6 8	1 4	1 0 0	0 16 8	3 4	2 0	2
2¼	2 7½	0 5 3	1 1 0	21 0 0	9 7 6	1 7	1 2 6	0 18 9	3 9	2 3	2¼
2½	2 11	0 5 10	1 3 4	23 6 8	10 8 4	1 10	1 5 0	1 0 10	4 2	2 6	2½
2¾	3 2½	0 6 5	1 5 8	25 13 4	11 9 2	1 13	1 7 6	1 2 11	4 7	2 9	2¾
3	3 6	0 7 0	1 8 0	28 0 0	12 10 0	1 16	1 10 6	1 5 0	5 2	3 0	3
3¼	3 9½	0 7 7	1 10 4	30 6 8	13 10 10	1 19	1 12 6	1 7 1	5 5	3 3	3¼
3½	4 1	0 8 2	1 12 8	32 13 4	14 11 8	2 2	1 15 0	1 9 2	5 10	3 6	3½
3¾	4 4½	0 8 9	1 15 0	35 0 0	15 12 6	2 5	1 17 6	1 11 3	6 3	3 9	3¾
4	4 8	0 9 4	1 17 4	37 6 8	16 13 4	2 8	2 0 0	1 13 4	6 8	4 0	4
4¼	4 11½	0 9 11	1 19 8	39 13 4	17 14 2	2 11	2 2 6	1 15 5	7 1	4 3	4¼
4½	5 3	0 10 6	2 2 0	42 0 0	18 15 0	2 14	2 5 0	1 17 6	7 6	4 6	4½
4¾	5 6½	0 11 1	2 4 4	44 6 8	19 15 10	2 17	2 7 6	1 19 7	7 11	4 9	4¾
5	5 10	0 11 8	2 6 8	46 13 4	20 16 8	3 0	2 10 0	2 1 8	8 4	5 0	5

5¼	6	1½	0	12	3	2	9	0	49	0	0	21	17	6	3	3	2	12	6	2	3	9	8	9	5	3	5¼
5½	6	5	0	12	10	2	11	4	51	6	8	22	18	4	3	6	2	15	0	2	5	10	9	2	5	6	5½
5¾	6	8½	0	13	5	2	13	8	53	13	4	23	19	2	3	9	2	17	6	2	7	11	9	7	5	9	5¾
6	7	0	0	14	0	2	16	0	56	0	0	25	0	0	3	12	3	0	0	2	10	0	10	0	6	0	6
6¼	7	3½	0	14	7	2	18	4	58	6	8	26	0	10	3	15	3	2	6	2	12	1	10	5	6	3	6¼
6½	7	7	0	15	2	3	0	8	60	13	4	27	1	8	3	18	3	5	0	2	14	2	10	10	6	6	6½
6¾	7	10½	0	15	9	3	3	0	63	0	0	28	2	6	4	1	3	7	6	2	16	3	11	3	6	9	6¾
7	8	2	0	16	5	3	5	4	65	6	8	29	3	4	4	4	3	10	0	2	18	4	11	8	7	0	7.
7¼	8	5½	0	16	11	3	7	8	67	13	4	30	4	2	4	7	3	12	6	3	0	5	12	1	7	3	7¼
7½	8	9	0	17	6	3	10	0	70	0	0	31	5	0	4	10	3	15	0	3	2	6	12	6	7	6	7½
7¾	9	0½	0	18	1	3	12	4	72	6	8	32	5	10	4	13	3	17	6	3	4	7	12	11	7	9	7¾
8	9	4	0	18	8	3	14	8	74	13	4	33	6	8	4	16	4	0	0	3	6	8	13	4	8	0	8
8¼	9	7½	0	19	3	3	17	0	77	0	0	34	7	6	4	19	4	2	6	3	8	9	13	9	8	3	8¼
8½	9	11	0	19	10	3	19	4	79	6	8	35	8	4	5	2	4	5	0	3	10	10	14	2	8	6	8½
8¾	10	2½	1	0	5	4	1	8	81	13	4	36	9	2	5	5	4	7	6	3	12	11	14	7	8	9	8¾
9	10	6	1	1	0	4	4	0	84	0	0	37	10	0	5	8	4	10	0	3	15	0	15	0	9	0	9
9¼	10	9½	1	1	7	4	6	4	86	6	8	38	10	10	5	11	4	12	6	3	17	1	15	5	9	3	9¼
9½	11	1	1	2	2	4	8	8	88	13	4	39	11	8	5	14	4	15	0	3	19	2	15	10	9	6	9½
9¾	11	4½	1	2	9	4	11	0	91	0	0	40	12	6	5	17	4	17	6	4	1	3	16	3	9	9	9¾
10	11	8	1	3	4	4	13	4	93	6	8	41	13	4	6	0	5	0	0	4	3	4	16	8	10	0	10
10¼	11	11½	1	3	11	4	15	8	95	13	4	42	14	2	6	3	5	2	6	4	5	5	17	1	10	3	10¼
10½	12	3	1	4	6	4	18	0	98	0	0	43	15	0	6	6	5	5	0	4	7	6	17	6	10	6	10½
10¾	12	6½	1	5	1	5	0	4	100	6	8	44	15	10	6	9	5	7	6	4	9	7	17	11	10	9	10¾
11	12	10	1	5	8	5	2	8	102	13	4	45	16	8	6	12	5	10	0	4	11	8	18	4	11	0	11
11¼	13	1½	1	6	3	5	5	0	105	0	0	46	17	6	6	15	5	12	6	4	13	9	18	9	11	3	11¼
11½	13	5	1	6	10	5	7	4	107	6	8	47	18	4	6	18	5	15	0	4	15	10	19	2	11	6	11½
11¾	13	8½	1	7	5	5	9	8	109	13	4	48	19	2	7	1	5	17	6	4	17	11	19	7	11	9	11¾
12	14	0	1	8	0	5	12	0	112	0	0	50	0	0	7	4	6	0	0	5	0	0	20	0	12	0	12

Table specifying the value of Moneys of Account of the principal places with which Britain has exchange transactions, taking silver at an estimated value of five shillings per ounce Troy.

Place	Money of account	Are equal to	is equal to in S. & D. British (S.)	(D.)	and giving for one £ sterling.
Amsterdam	100 centimes...	1 florin	1	8	11 flor. 97 cents...
Antwerp	The same as	Amsterdam.			
Berlin	30 sil. groschen	1 Pruss. dollar ...	2	10¾	6 doll. 27 s. g. ...
China	10 mace	1 tael	6	8	3 tael ....
Constantinople ..	40 paras	1 piastras	0	2¼	110 piastre ....
Copenhagen......	96 skillings ...	1 Reig. dollar......	2	2¼	9 doll. 10 sk. ......
Frankfort	24½ guilders ...	1 mark	1	7⅞	$12\frac{3}{40}$ guilders ......
Genoa	100 centisimi ..	1 lira Nuova	0	9½	15 li. 57 cents ....
Hamburg	16 schillings ...	1 mark	1	5½	13 mks. 10½ sch....
Havanna	100 cents.	1 dollar	4	6	4 doll. 44 cents....
Leghorn	100 centisimi ..	1 lira Toscana ...	0	8	30 li. 69 cents. ...
Lisbon	1000 reis	1 milreis	4	8	4 mil. 285 reis. ...
Madrid...	8 reals	1 dollar of plate...	3	1¾	6 doll. 2¾ reals ....
Malta	12 tari	1 scudi	1	8	12 scudo ....
New York.........	100 cents.	1 dollar	4	2	4 doll. 80 cents ...
Paris	100 centimes...	1 franc...............	0	9½	25 fr. 57 cents ....
Petersburg	100 copecks ...	1 rouble	3	1½	6 roub. 40 cop. ...
Rio Janeiro	1000 reis	1 milreis	2	7	7 mil. 117 reis ....
Venice	100 centisimi ..	1 lira Austriaca...	0	$8\frac{1}{13}$	29 li. 52 cents ....
Vienna...	60 krewzers ...	1 florin	2	$0\frac{4}{10}$	9 flor. 50 kr. ......

INDEX.

ENGINEERING, ARCHITECTURAL, MECHANICAL, AND SCIENTIFIC WORKS,

PUBLISHED BY

LOCKWOOD & CO.,

7, STATIONERS' HALL COURT, LUDGATE HILL.

The Year Book of Facts in Science and Art. Exhibiting the most important Improvements and Discoveries of the past year in Mechanics and the Useful Arts, Natural Philosophy, Electricity, Chemistry, Zoology and Botany, Geology and Mineralogy, Meteorology and Astronomy. By JOHN TIMBS, F.S.A. (Published annually.) Fcap. 5*s.* cloth.

*** This work records the proceedings of the principal scientific societies, and is indispensable for such as wish to possess a faithful picture of the latest novelties of science and the arts.

The High-Pressure Steam-Engine. By DR. ERNST ALBAN, Practical Machine Maker, Plau Mecklenberg. Translated from the German, by WILLIAM POLE, C.E., F.R.A.S., Assoc. Inst. C.E. 8vo, with 28 fine Plates, 16*s.* 6*d.* cloth.

A Practical and Theoretical Essay on Oblique Bridges. With 13 large Folding Plates. By GEORGE W. BUCK, M. Inst. C.E. Second Edition, corrected by W. H. BARLOW, M. Inst. C.E. Imperial 8vo, 12*s.* cloth.

The Practical Railway Engineer. By G. DRYSDALE DEMPSEY, Civil Engineer. Fourth Edition, Revised and greatly extended. With 71 double quarto Plates, 72 Woodcuts, and Portrait of G. STEPHENSON. One large Vol. 4to, £2 12*s.* 6*d.* cloth.

On Iron Ship-Building; with Practical Examples and Details, in Twenty-four Plates, together with Text containing Descriptions, Explanations, and General Remarks. By JOHN GRANTHAM, C.E., Consulting Engineer, and Naval Architect. Third Edition, Atlas of Plates, with separate Text, price £1 5*s.*

The Commercial Handbook of Chemical Analysis; or, Practical Instructions for the Determination of the Intrinsic or Commercial Value of Substances used in Manufactures, in Trades, and in the Arts. By Dr. A. NORMANDY. Post 8vo, illustrated with Woodcuts, 12*s.* 6*d.* cloth.

Practical Rules on Drawing, for the Operative Builder and Young Student in Architecture. By GEORGE PYNE, Author of "A Rudimentary Treatise on Perspective for Beginners." With 14 Plates, 4to, 7*s*. 6*d*. boards.

A Treatise on Ventilation, Natural and Artificial. By ROBERT RITCHIE, C.E., Author of "Railways—their Rise, Progress, and Construction;" "The Farm Engineer," and various Prize Essays on the Ventilation of Factories, Ships, etc. With numerous Plates and Woodcuts, 8vo, 8*s*. 6*d*. cloth.

The Operative Mechanic's Workshop Companion. Comprising a great variety of the most useful Rules in Mechanical Science, with numerous Tables of Practical Data and Calculated Results. By W. TEMPLETON, Author of "The Engineer's, Millwright's, and Mechanic's Practical Assistant," etc. 7th Edition, with 11 Plates. 12mo, price 5*s*., bound and lettered.

The Engineer's, Millwright's and Machinist's Practical Assistant; comprising a Collection of Useful Tables, Rules, and Data, compiled and arranged, with Original Matter, by WILLIAM TEMPLETON, Author of "The Operative Mechanic's Workshop Companion," etc. Second Edition, 18mo, 2*s*. 6*d*. cloth.

A Handy Book of Villa Architecture, being a Series of Designs for Villa Residences, in Various Styles. By C. WICKES, Architect, Author of "The Spires and Towers of the Mediæval Churches of England," etc. etc. First Series and Second Series. 4to, £1 7*s*. each, half morocco; or complete in 1 Vol. £2 10*s*. half morocco.

The Annual Retrospect of Engineering and Architecture; a Record of Progress in the Sciences of Civil, Military, and Naval Construction. Edited by GEORGE R. BURNELL, C.E., F.G.S., F.S.A. Vol. 1—January to December, 1861. Post 8vo, 7*s*. 6*d*. cloth.

Chambers' Civil Architecture, by Gwilt and Leeds.—A TREATISE ON THE DECORATIVE PART OF CIVIL ARCHITECTURE. By Sir WILLIAM CHAMBERS, K.P.S., F.R.S., F.S.A., F.S.S.S. With Illustrations, Notes, and an Examination of Grecian Architecture, by JOSEPH GWILT, Architect, F.S.A. New and Cheap Edition. Revised and edited by W. H. LEEDS. With 65 Plates, and Portrait of the Author. 4to, £1 1*s*. cloth.

Curiosities of Science, Past and Present. By JOHN TIMBS, F.S.A., Author of "Things not Generally Known," etc., etc. First and Second Series. Fcap., 2*s*. 6*d*. each, cloth.

www.ingramcontent.com/pod-product-compliance
Lightning Source LLC
Chambersburg PA
CBHW060946050726
47592CB00003B/1124

* 9 7 8 0 3 4 3 7 2 1 3 0 5 *